On the Trail

An Outdoor Book for Girls

Lina Beard and Adelia Belle Beard

TO ALL GIRLS
WHO LOVE THE LIFE OF THE OPEN
WE DEDICATE THIS BOOK

Over-night camp.
Fire notice is posted on tree.

TABLE OF CONTENTS

I. TRAILING
II. WOODCRAFT
III. CAMPING
IV. WHAT TO WEAR ON THE TRAIL
V. OUTDOOR HANDICRAFT
VI. MAKING FRIENDS WITH THE OUTDOOR FOLK
VII. WILD FOOD ON THE TRAIL
VIII. LITTLE FOES OF THE TRAILER
IX. ON THE TRAIL WITH YOUR CAMERA
X. ON AND IN THE WATER
XI. USEFUL KNOTS AND HOW TO TIE THEM
XII. ACCIDENTS
XIII. CAMP FUN AND FROLICS
XIV. HAPPY AND SANE SUNDAY IN CAMP

PRESENTATION

The joyous, exhilarating call of the wilderness and the forest camp is surely and steadily penetrating through the barriers of brick, stone, and concrete; through the more or less artificial life of town and city; and the American girl is listening eagerly. It is awakening in her longings for free, wholesome, and adventurous outdoor life, for the innocent delights of nature-loving Thoreau and bird-loving Burroughs. Sturdy, independent, self-reliant, she is now demanding outdoor books that are genuine and filled with practical information; books that tell how to do worth-while things, that teach real woodcraft and are not adapted to the girl supposed to be afraid of a caterpillar or to shudder at sight of a harmless snake.

In answer to the demand, "On the Trail" has been written. The authors' deep desire is to help girls respond to this new, insistent call by pointing out to them the open trail. It is their hope and wish that their girl readers may seek the charm of the wild and may find the same happiness in the life of the open that the American boy has enjoyed since the first settler built his little cabin on the shores of the New World. To forward this object, the why and how, the where and when of things of camp and trail have been embodied in this book.

Thanks are due to Edward Cave, president and editor of Recreation, for kindly allowing the use of some of his wild-life photographs.

Lina Beard,
Adelia Belle Beard.
Flushing, N. Y.,
March 16, 1915.

ON THE TRAIL

CHAPTER I
TRAILING
What the Outdoor World Can Do for Girls.
How to Find the Trail and How to Keep It

There is a something in you, as in every one, every man, woman, girl, and boy, that requires the tonic life of the wild. You may not know it, many do not, but there is a part of your nature that only the wild can reach, satisfy, and develop. The much-housed, overheated, overdressed, and over-entertained life of most girls is artificial, and if one does not turn away from and leave it for a while, one also becomes greatly artificial and must go through life not knowing the joy, the strength, the poise that real outdoor life can give.

What is it about a true woodsman that instantly compels our respect, that sets him apart from the men who might be of his class in village or town and puts him in a class by himself, though he may be exteriorly rough and have little or no book education? The real Adirondack or the North Woods guide, alert, clean-limbed, clear-eyed, hard-muscled, bearing his pack-basket or duffel-bag on his back, doing all the hard work of the camp, never loses his poise or the simple dignity which he shares with all the things of the wild. It is bred in him, is a part of himself and the life he leads. He is as conscious of his superior knowledge of the woods as an astronomer is of his knowledge of the stars, and patiently tolerates the ignorance and awkwardness of the "tenderfoot" from the city. Only a keen sense of humor can make this toleration possible, for I have seen things done by a city-dweller at camp that would enrage a woodsman, unless the irresistibly funny side of it made him laugh his inward laugh that seldom reaches the surface.

To live for a while in the wild strengthens the muscles of your mind as well as of your body. Flabby thoughts and flabby muscles depart together and are replaced by enthusiasm and vigor of purpose, by strength of limb and chest and back. To *have* seems not so desirable as to *be*. When you have once come into sympathy with this world of the wild—which holds our cultivated, artificial world in the hollow of its hand and gives it life—new joy, good, wholesome, heartfelt joy, will well up within you. New and absorbing interests will claim your attention. You will breathe deeper, stand straighter. The small, petty things of life will lose their seeming importance and great things will look larger and infinitely more worth while. You will know that the woods, the fields, the streams and great waters bear wonderful messages for you, and, little by little, you will learn to read them.

The majority of people who visit the up-to-date hotels of the Adirondacks, which their wily proprietors call camps, may think they see the wild and are living in it. But for them it is only a big picnic-ground through which they rush with unseeing eyes and whose cloisters they invade with unfeeling hearts, seemingly for the one purpose of building a fire, cooking their lunch, eating it, and then hurrying back to the comforts of the hotel and the gayety of hotel life.

One can generally pass around obstructions like this on the trail.
At their careless and noisy approach the forest suddenly withdraws itself into its deep reserve and reveals no secrets. It is as if they entered an empty house and passed through deserted rooms, but all the time the intruders are stealthily watched by unseen, hostile, or frightened eyes. Every form of moving life is stilled and magically fades into its background. The tawny rabbit halts amid the dry leaves of a fallen tree. No one sees it. The sinuous weasel slips silently under a rock by the side of the trail and is unnoticed. The mother grouse crouches low amid the underbrush and her little ones follow her example, but the careless company has no time to observe and drifts quickly by. Only the irrepressible red squirrel might be seen, but isn't, when he loses his balance and drops to a lower branch in his efforts to miss nothing of the excitement of the invasion.
This is not romance, it is truth. To think sentimentally about nature, to sit by a babbling brook and try to put your supposed feelings into verse, will not help you to know the wild. The only way to cultivate the sympathy and understanding which will enable you to feel its heart-beats, is to go to it humbly, ready to see the wonders it can show; ready to appreciate and love its beauties and ready to meet on friendly and cordial terms the animal life whose home it is. The wild world is, indeed, a wonderful world; how wonderful and interesting we learn only by degrees and actual experience. It is free, but not lawless; to enter it fully we must obey these laws which are slowly and silently impressed upon us. It is a wholesome, life-giving, inspiring world, and when you have learned to conform to its rules you are met on every hand by friendly messengers to guide you and teach you the ways of the wild: wild birds, wild fruits and plants, and gentle, furtive, wild animals. You cannot put their messages into words, but you can feel them; and then, suddenly, you no longer care for soft cushions and rugs, for shaded lamps, dainty fare and finery, for paved streets and concrete walks. You want to plant your feet upon the earth in its natural state, however rugged or boggy it may be. You want your cushions to be of the soft moss-beds of the piny woods, and, with the unparalleled sauce of a healthy, hearty appetite, you want to eat your dinner

out of doors, cooked over the outdoor fire, and to drink water from a birch-bark cup, brought cool and dripping from the bubbling spring.

You want, oh! how you want to sleep on a springy bed of balsam boughs, wrapped in soft, warm, woollen blankets with the sweet night air of all outdoors to breathe while you sleep. You want your flower-garden, not with great and gorgeous masses of bloom in evident, orderly beds, but keeping always charming surprises for unexpected times and in unsuspected places. You want the flowers that grow without your help in ways you have not planned; that hold the enchantment of the wilderness. Some people are born with this love for the wild, some attain it, but in either case the joy is there, and to find it you must seek it. Your chosen trail may lead through the primeval forests or into the great western deserts or plains; or it may reach only left-over bits of the wild which can be found at no great distance from home. Even a bit of meadow or woodland, even an uncultivated field on the hilltop, will give you a taste of the wild; and if you strike the trail in the right spirit you will find upon arrival that these remnants of the wild world have much to show and to teach you. There are the sky, the clouds, the lungfuls of pure air, the growing things which send their roots where they will and not in a man-ordered way. There is the wild life that obeys no man's law: the insects, the birds, and small four-footed animals. On all sides you will find evidences of wild life if you will look for it. Here you may make camp for a day and enjoy that day as much as if it were one of many in a several weeks' camping trip.

However, this is not to be a book of glittering generalities but, as far as it can be made, one of practical helpfulness in outdoor life; therefore when you are told to strike the trail you must also be told how to do it.

When You Strike the Trail

For any journey, by rail or by boat, one has a general idea of the direction to be taken, the character of the land or water to be crossed, and of what one will find at the end. So it should be in striking the trail. Learn all you can about the path you are to follow. Whether it is plain or obscure, wet or dry; where it leads; and its length, measured more by time than by actual miles. A smooth, even trail of five miles will not consume the time and strength that must be expended upon a trail of half that length which leads over uneven ground, varied by bogs and obstructed by rocks and fallen trees, or a trail that is all up-hill climbing. If you are a novice and accustomed to walking only over smooth and level ground, you must allow more time for covering the distance than an experienced person would require and must count upon the expenditure of more strength, because your feet are not trained to the wilderness paths with their pitfalls and traps for the unwary, and every nerve and muscle will be strained to secure a safe foothold amid the tangled roots, on the slippery, moss-covered logs, over precipitous rocks that lie in your path. It will take time to pick your way over boggy places where the water oozes up through the thin, loamy soil as through a sponge; and experience alone will teach you which hummock of grass or moss will make a safe stepping-place and will not sink beneath your weight and soak your feet with hidden water. Do not scorn to learn all you can about the trail you are to take, although your questions may call forth superior smiles. It is not that you hesitate to encounter difficulties, but that you may prepare for them. In unknown regions take a responsible guide with you, unless the trail is short, easily followed, and a frequented one. Do not go alone through lonely places; and, being on the trail, keep it and try no explorations of your own, at least not until you are quite familiar with the country and the ways of the wild.

Difficulties of the Adirondack trail.

Facsimile of drawing made by a trailer (not the author) after a day in the wilds of an Adirondack forest. Not a good drawing, perhaps, but a good illustration.

Blazing the Trail
A woodsman usually blazes his trail by chipping with his axe the trees he passes, leaving white scars on their trunks, and to follow such a trail you stand at your first tree until you see the blaze on the next, then go to that and look for the one farther on; going in this way from tree to tree you keep the trail though it may, underfoot, be overgrown and indistinguishable.

If you must make a trail of your own, blaze it as you go by bending down and breaking branches of trees, underbrush, and bushes. Let the broken branches be on the side of bush or tree in the direction you are going, but bent down away from that side, or toward the bush, so that the lighter underside of the leaves will show and make a plain trail. Make these signs conspicuous and close together, for in returning, a dozen feet without the broken branch will sometimes confuse you, especially as everything has a different look when seen from the opposite side. By this same token it is a wise precaution to look back frequently as you go and impress the homeward-bound landmarks on your memory. If in your wanderings you have branched off and made ineffectual or blind trails which lead nowhere, and, in returning to camp, you are led astray by one of them, do not leave the false trail and strike out to make a new one, but turn back and follow the false trail to its beginning, for it must lead to the true trail again. *Don't lose sight of your broken branches.*

Blazing the trail by bending down and breaking branches.

If you carry a hatchet or small axe you can make a permanent trail by blazing the trees as the woodsmen do. Kephart advises blazing in this way: make one blaze on the side of the tree away from the camp and two blazes on the side toward the camp. Then when you return you look for the *one* blaze. In leaving camp again to follow the same trail, you look for the *two* blazes. If you should lose the trail and reach it again you will know to a certainty which direction to take, for two blazes mean *camp on this side*; one blaze, *away from camp on this side*.

To Know an Animal Trail
To know an animal trail from one made by men is quite important. It is easy to be led astray by animal trails, for they are often well defined and, in some cases, well beaten. To the uninitiated the trails will appear the same, but there is a difference which, in a recent number of *Field and Stream*, Mr. Arthur Rice defines very clearly in this way: "Men step *on* things. Animals step *over* or around things." Then again an animal trail frequently passes under bushes and low branches of trees where men would cut or break their way through. To follow an animal trail is to be led sometimes to water, often to a bog or swamp, at times to the animal's den, which in the case of a bear might not be exactly pleasant.

Returning to camp by the blazed trail.
Note the blazed trees.

Lost in the Woods

We were in the wilderness of an Adirondack forest making camp for the day and wanted to see the beaver-dam which, we were told, was on the edge of a near-by lake. The guide was busy cooking dinner and we would not wait for his leisure, but leaving the rest of the party, we started off confidently, just two of us, down the perfectly plain trail. For a short distance there was a beaten path, then, suddenly, the trail came to an abrupt end. We looked this side and that. No trail, no appearance of there ever having been one. With a careless wave of his arm, the guide had said: "Keep in that direction." "That" being to the left, to the left we therefore turned and stormed our way through thicket and bramble, breaking branches as we went. Sliding down declivities, scrambling over fallen trees, dipping beneath low-hung branches, we finally came out upon the shore of the lake and found that we had struck the exact spot where the beaver-dam was located. It was only a short distance from camp and it had not taken us long to make it, but when we turned back we warmly welcomed the sight of our blazed trail, for all else was strange and unfamiliar. Going there had been glimpses of the water now and then to guide us, returning we had no landmarks. Even my sense of direction, usually to be relied on and upon which I had been tempted to depend solely, seemed to play me false when we reached a place where our blazing was lost sight of. The twilight stillness of the great forest enveloped us; there was no sign of our camp, no sound of voices. A few steps to our left the ground fell away in a steep precipice which, in going, we had passed unnoticed and which, for the moment, seemed to obstruct our way. Then turning to the right we saw a streak of light through the trees that looked, at first, like water where we felt sure no water could be if we were on the right path; but we soon recognized this as smoke kept in a low cloud by the trees—the smoke of our camp-fire. That was our beacon, and we were soon on the trail again and back in camp. This is not told as an adventure, but to illustrate the fact that without a well-blazed trail it is easier to become lost in a strange forest than to find one's way.

You may strike the trail with the one object in view of reaching your destination as quickly as possible. This will help you to become agile and sure-footed, to cover long distances in a short time, but it will not allow of much observation until your mind has become alert and your eyes trained to see quickly the things of the forests and plains, and to read their signs correctly. Unless there is necessity for haste, it is better to take more time and look about you as you go. To hurry over the trail is to lose much that is of interest and to pass by unseeingly things of great beauty. When you are new to the trail and must hurry, you are intent only on what is just before you—usually the feet of your guide—or if you raise your eyes to glance ahead, you notice objects simply as things to be reached and passed as quickly as possible. Unhurried trailing will repay you by showing you what the world of the wild contains.

Walking slowly you can realize the solemn stillness of the forest, can take in the effect of the gray light which enfolds all things like a veil of mystery. You can stop to examine the tiny-leafed, creeping vines that cover the ground like moss and the structure of the soft mosses with fronds like ferns. You can catch the jewel-like gleam of the wood flowers. You can breathe deeply and rejoice in the perfume of the balsam and pine. You can rest at intervals and wait quietly for evidences of the animal life that you know is lurking, unseen, all around you; and you can begin to perceive the protecting spirit of the wild that hovers over all.

To walk securely, as the woodsmen walk, without tripping, stumbling, or slipping, use the woodsmen's method of planting the entire foot on the ground, with toes straight ahead, not turned out. If you put your heel down first, while crossing on a slippery log as in ordinary walking, the natural result will be a fall. With your entire foot as a base upon which to rest, the body is more easily balanced and the foot less likely to slip. When people slip and fall on the ice, it is because the edge of the heel strikes the ice first and slides. The whole foot on the ice would not slip in the same way, and very often not at all.

Trailing does not consist merely in walking along a path or in making one for yourself. It has a larger meaning than that and embraces various lines of outdoor life, while it always presupposes movement of some kind. In one sense going on the trail means going on the hunt. You may go on the trail for birds, for animals, for insects, plants, or flowers. You may trail a party of friends ahead of you, or follow a deer to its drinking-place; and in all these cases you must look for the signs of that which you seek.

Footprints or Tracks

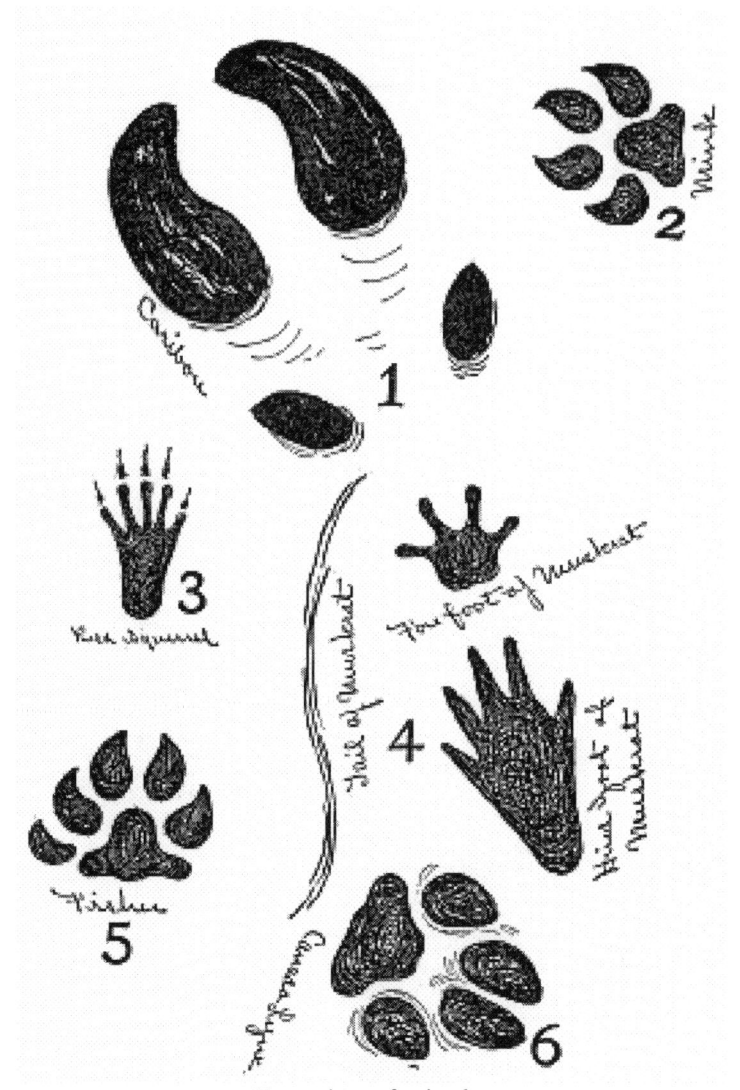

Footprints of animals.

In trailing animals look for footprints in soft earth, sand, or snow. The hind foot of the muskrat will leave a print in the mud like that of a little hand, and with it will be the forefoot print, showing but four short fingers, and generally the streaks where the hard tail drags behind. Fig. 4 shows what these look like. If you are familiar with the dog track you will know something about the footprints of the fox, wolf, and coyote, for they are much alike. Fig. 9 gives a clean track of the fox, but often there is the imprint of hairs between and around the toes. A wolf track is larger and is like Fig. 8. The footprint of a deer shows the cloven hoof, with a difference between the buck's and the doe's. The doe's toes are pointed and, when not spread, the track is almost heart-shaped (Fig. 7), while the buck has blunter, more rounded toes, like Fig. 10. The two round lobes are at the back of the foot, the other end points in the direction the deer has taken. Sometimes you will find deer tracks with the toes spread wide apart. That means the animal has been running. All animals' toes spread more or less when they run. A bear track is like Fig. 11, but a large bear often leaves other evidences of his presence than his footprints. He will frequently turn a big log over or tear one open in his search for ants. He will stand on his hind legs and gnaw a hole in a dead tree or tall stump, and a bee-tree will bear the marks of his climbing on its trunk. It is interesting to find a tree with the scars of bruin's feet, made prominent by small knobs where his claws have sunk into the bark. Each scar swells and stands out like one of his toes. When you see bark scraped off the trees some distance from the ground, you may be sure that a horned animal has passed that way. Where the trees are not far apart a wide-horned animal, like the bull moose, scrapes the bark with his antlers as he passes.

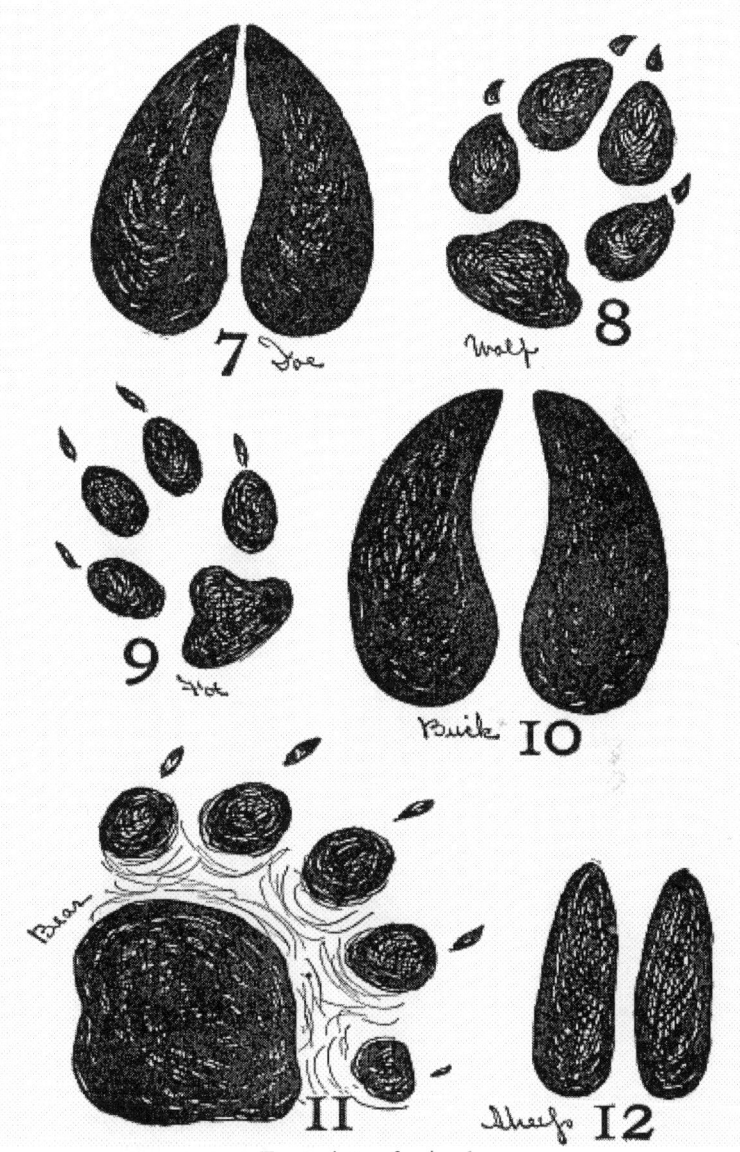

Footprints of animals.

The cat-like lynx leaves a cat-like track (Fig. 6), which shows no print of the claws, and the mink's track is like Fig. 2. Rabbits' tracks are two large oblongs, then two almost round marks. The oblongs are the print of the large hind feet, which, with the peculiar gait of the rabbit, always come first. The large, hind-feet tracks point the direction the animal has taken. Fig. 1 is the track of the caribou, and shows the print of the dew-claws, which are the two little toes up high at the back of the foot. It is when the earth is soft and the foot sinks in deeply that the dew-claws leave a print, or perhaps when the foot spreads wide in running. Fig. 3 is the print of the foot of a red squirrel. Fig. 5 is the fisher's track, and Fig. 12 is that of a sheep. Pig tracks are much like those of sheep, but wider. When you have learned to recognize the varying freshness of tracks you will know how far ahead the animal probably is. Other tracks you will learn as you become more familiar with the animals, and you will also be able to identify the tracks of the wild birds.

CHAPTER II
WOODCRAFT
Trees. Practical Use of Compass. Direction of Wind. Star Guiding. What to Do When Lost in the Woods. How to Chop Wood. How to Fell Trees.

Trees
While on the trail you will find a knowledge of trees most useful, and you should be able to recognize different species by their manner of growth, their bark and foliage.

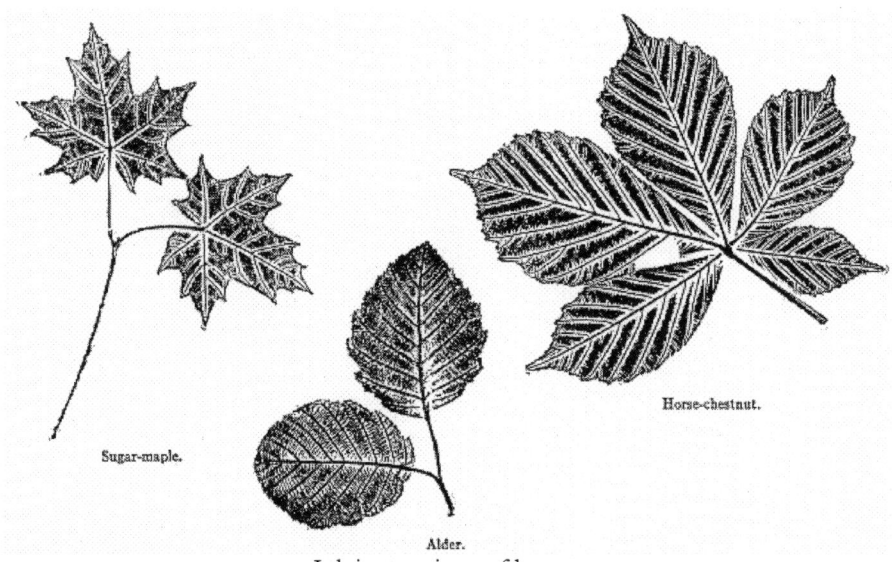

Ink impressions of leaves.

Balsam-Fir
One of the most important trees for the trailer to know is the balsam-fir, for of this the best of outdoor beds are made. In shape the tree is like our Christmas-trees—in fact, many Christmas-trees are balsam-fir.

The sweet, aromatic perfume of the balsam needles is a great aid in identifying it. The branches are flat and the needles appear to grow from the sides of the stem. The little twist at the base of the needle causes it to seem to grow merely in the straight, outstanding row on each side of the stem; look closely and you will see the twist.

The needles are flat and short, hardly one inch in length; they are grooved along the top and the ends are decidedly blunt; in color they are dark bluish-green on the upper side and silvery-white underneath. The bark is gray, and you will find little gummy blisters on the tree-trunk. From these the healing Canada balsam is obtained. The short cones, often not over two inches in length, the longest seldom more than four inches, stand erect on top of the small branches, and when young are of a purplish color.

From Maine to Minnesota the balsam-fir grows in damp woods and mountain bogs, and you will find it southward along the Alleghany Mountains from Pennsylvania to North Carolina.

Spruce
The spruce, red, black, and white, differs in many respects from the balsam-fir: the needles are sharp-pointed, not blunt, and instead of being flat like the balsam-fir, they are four-sided and cover the branchlet on all sides, causing it to appear rounded or bushy and not flat. The spruce-gum sought by many is found in the seams of the bark, which, unlike the smooth balsam-fir, is scaly and of a brown color. Early spring is the time to look for spruce-gum. Spruce is a soft wood, splits readily and is good for the frames and ribs of boats, also for paddles and oars, and the bark makes a covering for temporary shelters.

Hemlock
This tree is good for thatching a lean-to when balsam-fir is not to be found, and its bark can be used in the way of shingles.

The cones are small and hang down from the branches; they do not stand up alert like those of the balsam-fir, nor are they purple in color, being rather of a bright red-brown, and when very young, tan color. The wood is not easy to split—don't try it, or your hatchet will suffer in consequence and the pieces will be twisted as a usual thing. The southern variety, however, often splits straight.

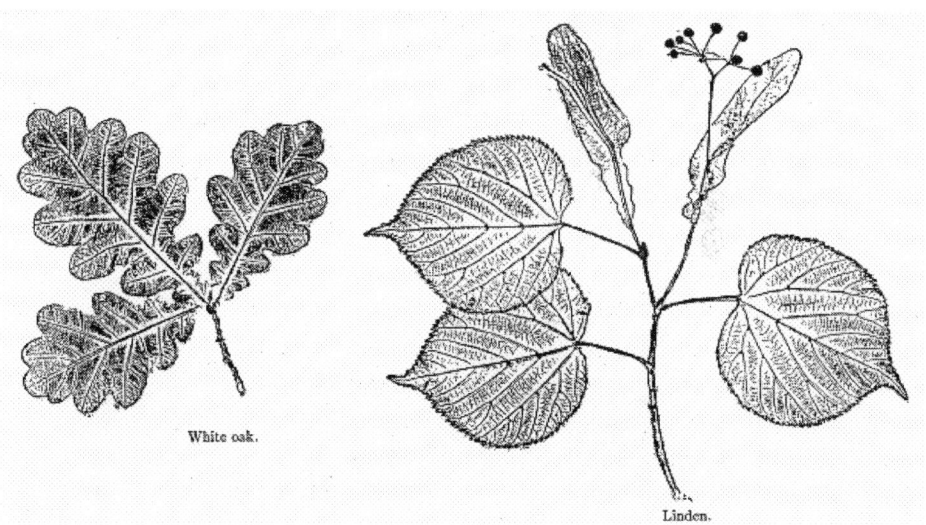

White oak.

Linden.

Ink impressions of leaves.

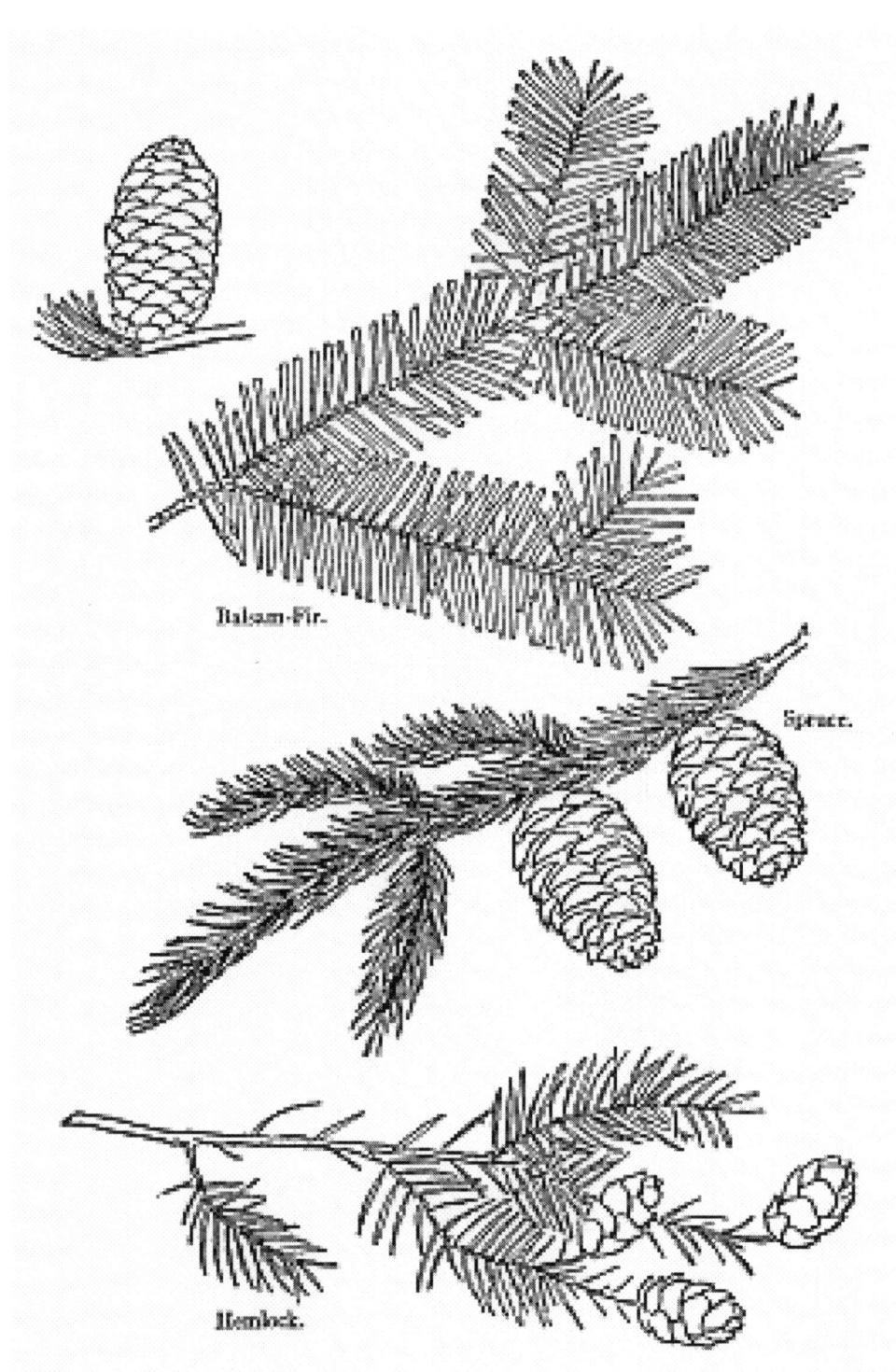

Balsam-Fir. Spruce. Hemlock.

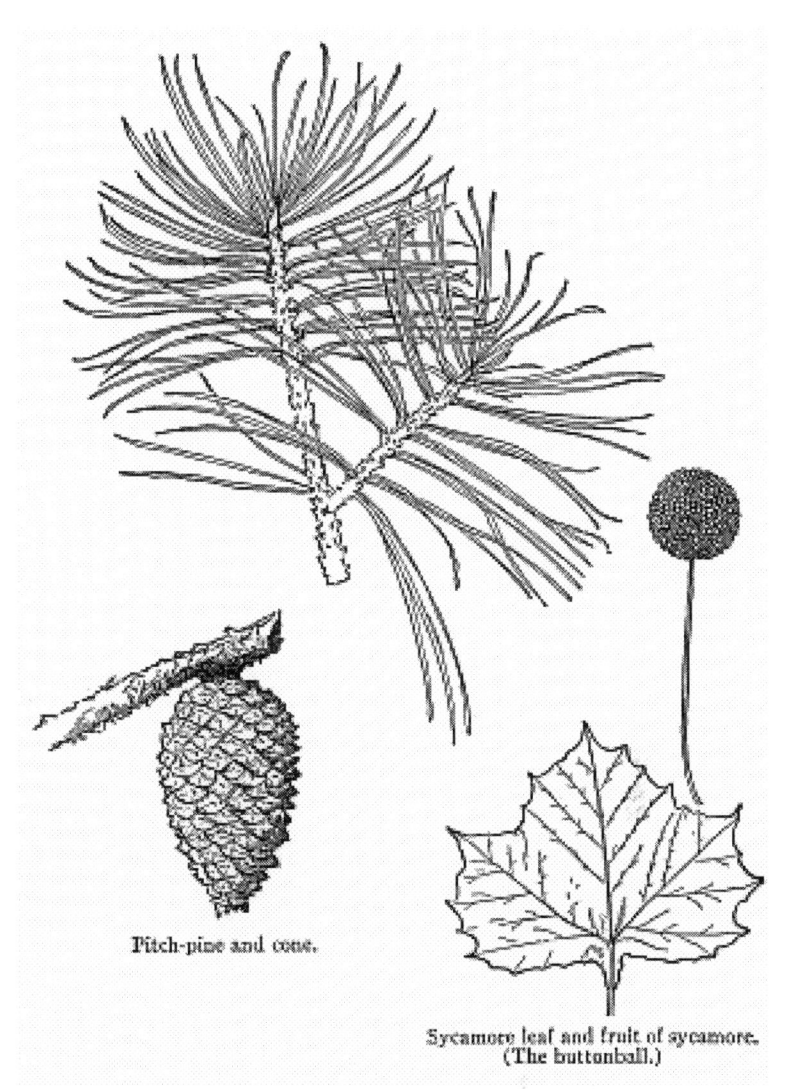

Pitch-pine and cone. Sycamore leaf and fruit of sycamore.

Pine

The pine-tree accommodates itself to almost any kind of soil, high, low, moist, or dry, often growing along the edge of the water.

The gray pine is sometimes used for making the skeleton of a canoe or other boats, and the white pine for the skin or covering of the skeleton boat; but for you the pine will probably be most useful in furnishing pine-knots, and its soft wood for kindling your outdoor fire.

The trees mentioned abound in our northern forests. The birch in its different varieties is there also, but rarely ventures into the densest woods, preferring to remain near and on its outskirts. However, none of these trees confine themselves strictly to one locality.

Oaks, hickory, chestnut, maples, and sycamore are among the useful woods for campers.

Learn the quality and nature of the different trees. Each variety is distinct from the others: some woods are easy to split, such as spruce, chestnut, balsam-fir, etc.; some very strong, as locust, oak, hickory, sugar-maple, etc.; then there are the hard and soft woods mentioned in fire-making.

When you once understand the characteristics of the different woods, and their special qualifications, becoming familiar with only two or three varieties at a time, the trees will be able to help you according to their special powers. You would not go to a musician to have a portrait painted, for while the musician might give you wonderful music he would be helpless as far as painting a picture was concerned, and so it is with trees. They cannot all give the same thing; if you want soft wood, it is wasting your time to go to hardwood trees; they cannot give you what they do not possess. Know the possibilities of trees and they will not fail you.

How to Chop Wood

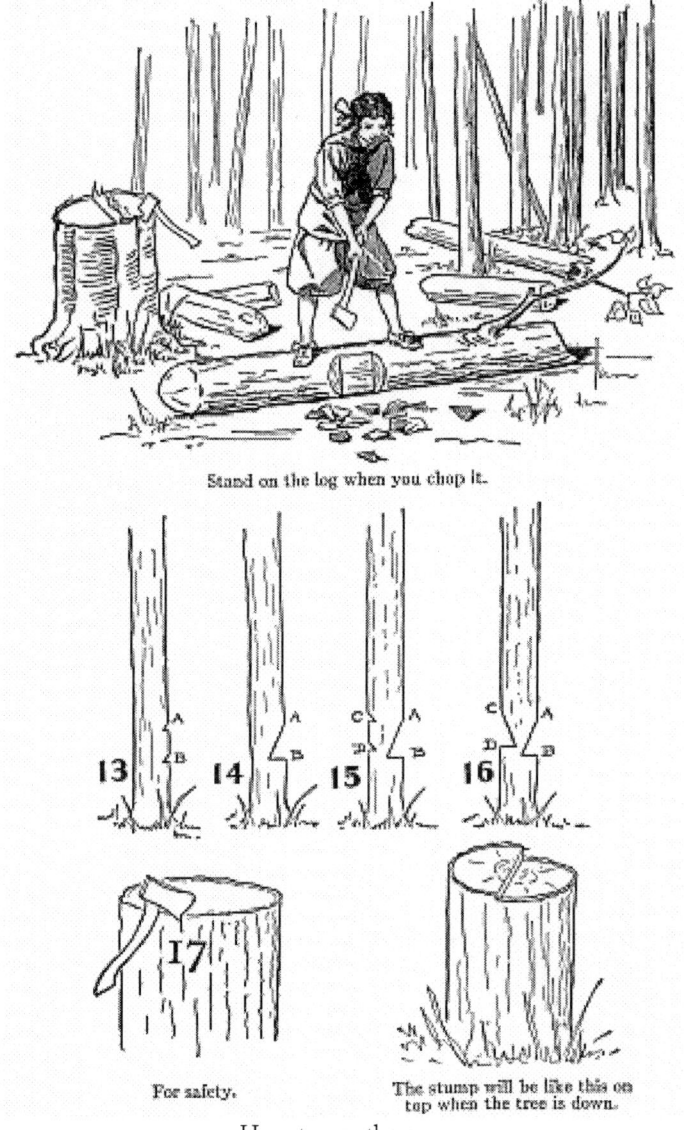

Stand on the log when you chop it.

For safety.

The stump will be like this on top when the tree is down.

How to use the axe.

Trailing and camping both mean wood-chopping to some extent for shelters, fires, etc., and the girl of to-day should understand, as did the girls of our pioneer families, how to handle properly a hatchet, or in this case we will make it a belt axe. There is a small hatchet modelled after the Daniel Boone tomahawk, generally known as the "camp axe." It is thicker, narrower, and has a sharper edge than an ordinary hatchet. It comes of a size to wear on the belt and must be securely protected by a well-fitted strong leather sheath; otherwise it will endanger not only the life of the girl who carries it, but also the lives of her companions. With the camp axe (hatchet) you can cut down small trees, chop firewood, blaze trees, drive down pegs or stakes, and chop kindling-wood. Every time you want to use the hatchet take the precaution to examine it thoroughly and reassure yourself that the tool is in good condition and that the *head* is *on firm* and *tight*; be positive of this.

Great caution must be taken when chopping kindling-wood, as often serious accidents occur through ignorance or carelessness. Do not raise one end of a stick up on a log with the other end down on the ground and then strike the centre of the stick a sharp blow with the sharp edge of your hatchet; the stick will break, but one end usually flies up with considerable force and very often strikes the eye of the worker, ruining the sight forever. Take the blunt end of your hatchet and do not give a very hard blow on the stick you wish to break; exert only force sufficient to break it partially, merely enough to enable you to finish the work with your hands and possibly one knee. It may require a little more time, but your eyes will be unharmed, which makes it worth while. Often children use a heavy stone to break kindling-wood, with no disastrous results that I know of. The heavy stone does not seem to cause the wood to fly upward.

How to Chop Logs
Practise on small, slender logs, chopping them in short lengths until you understand something of the woodsman's art of "logging up a tree"; then and not until then should you attempt to cut heavier wood.

If you are sure-footed and absolutely certain that you can stand firmly on the log without teetering or swaying when leaning over, do so. You can then chop one side of the log half-way through and turn around and chop the other side until the second notch or "kerf" is cut through to the first one on the opposite side, and the two pieces fall apart. While working stand on the log with feet wide apart and chop the *side* of the log (not the top) on the space in front between your feet. Make your first chip quite long, and have it equal in length the diameter of the log. If the chip is short, the opening of the kerf will be narrow and your hatchet will become wedged, obliging you to double your labor by enlarging the kerf. Greater progress will be made by chopping diagonally across the grain of the wood, and the work will be easier. It is difficult to cut squarely against the grain and this is always avoided when possible. After you have cut the first chip in logging up a tree, chop on the base of the chip, swinging your hatchet from the opposite direction, and the chip will fall to the ground.

Having successfully chopped off one piece of the log, it will be a simple matter to cut off more. Chop slowly, easily, and surely. Don't be in a hurry and exhaust yourself; only a novice overexerts and tries to make a deep cut with the hatchet. Be careful of the blade of your hatchet; keep it free from the ground when chopping, to avoid striking snags, stones, or other things liable to nick or dull the edge.

How to Fell a Tree
Content yourself with chopping down only slender trees, mere saplings, at first, and as you acquire skill, slightly heavier trees can be felled. Begin in the right way with your very first efforts and follow the woodsman's method.

Having selected the tree you desire to cut down, determine in which direction you want it to fall and mark that side, but first make sure that when falling, the tree will not lodge in another one near by or drop on one of the camp shelters. See that the way is free of hindrance before cutting the tree, also *clear the way* for the swing of your extended *hatchet*. If there are obstacles, such as vines, bushes, limbs of other trees, or rocks, which your hatchet might strike as you raise and lower it while at work, clear them all away, making a generous open space on all sides, overhead, on the right and left side, and below the swing of the hatchet. Take no chance of having an accident, as would occur should the hatchet become entangled or broken.

You may have noticed that the top surface of most stumps has a splintered ridge across its centre, and on one side of the ridge the wood is lower than on the other; this is because of the manner in which a woodsman fells a tree. If he wants the tree to fall toward the west he marks the west side of the trunk; then he marks the top and bottom of the space he intends chopping out for the first kerf or notch (Fig. 13, *A* and *B*), making the length of space a trifle longer than one-half of the tree diameter. The kerf is chopped out by cutting first from the top *A*, then from the bottom *B* (Fig. 14). When the first kerf is finished and cut half-way through the tree, space for the kerf on the opposite side of the tree is marked a few inches higher than the first one (Fig. 15, *C* and *D*) and then it also is cut (Fig. 16).

After you have chopped the two kerfs in a tree, you will know when it is about to fall by the creaking and the slight movement of its top. Step to *one side* of the falling tree, never behind or in front of it; either of the last two ways would probably mean death: if in front, the tree would fall on you, and if at the back, you would probably be terribly injured if not killed, as trees often kick backward with tremendous force as they go down; so be on your guard, keep cool, and deliberately step to the side of the tree and watch it fall.

Choose a quiet day, when there is no wind, for tree-felling. You cannot control the wind, and it may control your tree.

Never allow your hatchet to lie on the ground, a menace to every one at camp, but have a particular log or stump and always strike the blade in this wood. Leave your hatchet there, where it will not be injured, can do no harm, and you will always know where to find it (Fig. 17).

Etiquette of the Wild

Translated this means "*hands off.*" The unwritten law of the woods is that personal property cached in trees, underbrush, beneath stones, or hidden underground must never be *taken*, *borrowed*, *used*, or *molested*.

Canoes and oars will often be discovered left by owners, sometimes fastened at the water's edge, again suspended from trees, and the temptation to borrow may be strong, but remember such an act would be dishonorable and against the rules that govern the outdoor world.

Provisions, tools, or other articles found in the forests should be respected and allowed to remain where they are. It is customary for campers to cache their belongings with the assurance that forest etiquette will be held inviolate and their goods remain unmolested.

Every one has the privilege of examining and enjoying the beauties of mosses, berries, and wild flowers, but do not take these treasures from their homes to die and be thrown aside. Love them well enough to let them stay where they are for others also to enjoy, unless you need specimens for some important special study.

A man who had always lived in the Adirondack forests, and at present is proprietor of an Adirondack hotel, recently reforested many acres of his wooded wild lands by planting through the forests little young trees, some not over one foot high, and his indignation was great when he discovered that many of his guests when off on tramps returned laden with these baby trees, which were easily pulled up by the roots because so lately planted.

Finding Your Way by Natural Signs and the Compass

An important phase of woodcraft is the ability to find your way in the wilderness by means of natural signs as well as the compass. If, however, you do not know at what point of the compass from you the camp lies, the signs can be of no avail. Having this knowledge, the signs will be invaluable.

Get your bearings before leaving camp. Do not depend upon any member of the party, but know for yourself.

If you have a map giving the topography of land surrounding the camping-grounds, consult it. Burn into your memory the direction *from* camp of outlying landmarks, those near and those as far off as you can see in all directions. The morning you leave camp, ascertain the direction of the wind and notice particularly the sun and shadows. If it is early morning, face the sun and you will be looking toward the east. Stretch out both arms at your sides and point with your index-fingers; your right finger will point to the south, your left to the north, and your back will be toward the west. What landmarks do you see east of the camp? South? North? West? And from what point of the compass does the wind blow? If it comes from the west and you trail eastward, the wind will strike your back going away from camp and should strike your face returning, provided its direction does not change. Again, if you go east, your camp will lie west of you, and your homeward path must be westward. Consult your compass and know exactly which direction you take when leaving camp, and blaze your trail as you go, looking backward frequently to see how landmarks should appear as you face them returning.

With all these friends to guide you, first, the map; second, sun; third, shadows; fourth, wind; fifth, compass; sixth, your bent-twig blazing, there will be little, if any, danger of being lost. But you must constantly keep on the alert and refer frequently to these guides, especially when deflecting from the course first taken after leaving camp. At every turning, stop and take your bearings anew; you cannot be too careful.

These signs are for daylight; at night the North Star will be your guide.

Sunlight and Shadow

Bearing in mind that the sun rises in the east and sets in the west, it will be comparatively easy to keep your right course by consulting the sun. A fair idea may also be gained of the time of day by the length of shadows, if you remember that shadows are long in the morning and continue to grow shorter until midday, when they again begin to lengthen, growing longer and longer until night.

To find the direction of the sun on a cloudy day, hold a flat splinter or your knife blade vertically, so that it is absolutely straight up and down. Place the point of the blade on your thumb-nail, watch-case, or other glossy surface; then turn the knife or splinter around until the full shadow of the flat of blade or splinter falls on the bright surface, telling the location of the sun.

An open spot where the sun can cast a clear shadow, and an hour when the sun is not immediately overhead, will give best results.

Wind

The wind generally blows in the same direction all day, and if you learn to understand its ways, the wind will help you keep the right trail. Make a practise of testing the direction of the wind every morning. Notice the leaves on bush and tree, in what direction they move. Place a few bits of paper on your open hand and watch in which way the wind carries them; if there is no paper, try the test with dry leaves, grass, or anything light and easily carried by the breeze. Smoke will also show the direction of the wind.

When the wind is very faint, put your finger in your mouth, wet it on all sides, and hold it up; the side on which the wind blows will feel cool and tell from what quarter the wind comes: if on the east side of your finger, the wind blows from the east, and so on. Keep testing the direction of the wind as you trail, and if at any time it cools a different side of the finger, you will know that you are not walking in the same direction as when you left camp and must turn until the wet finger tells you which way to go. The wind is a good guide so long as it keeps blowing in the same direction as when you left camp.

Use of Compass
Should you be on the trail and sudden storm-clouds appear, the sun cannot help you find your way; the shadows have gone. Moss on tree-trunks is not an infallible guide and you must turn to the compass to show the way, but unless you understand its language you will not know what it is telling you. Learn the language before going to camp; it is not difficult.

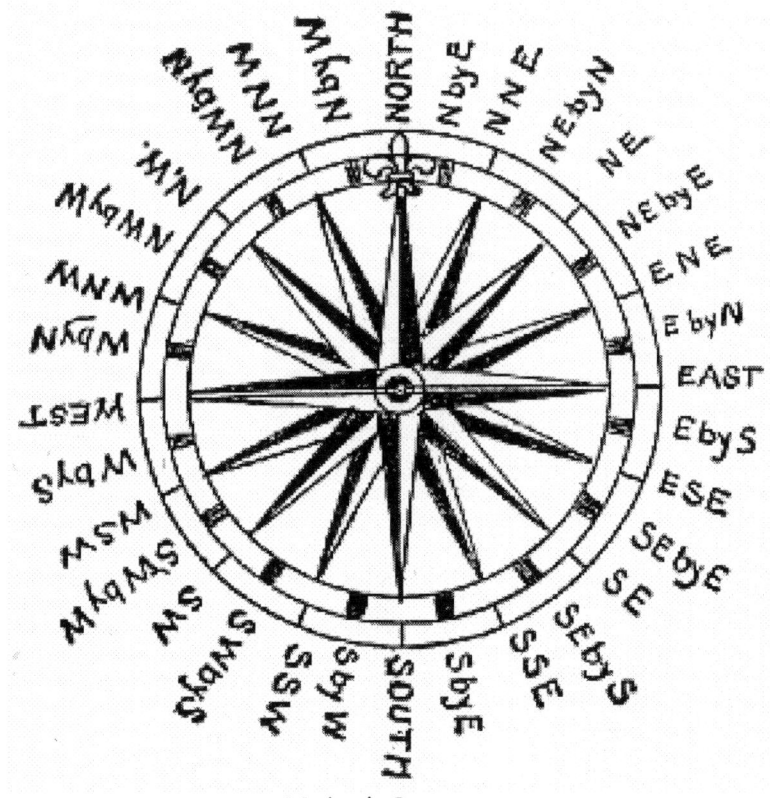

Mariner's Compass.

Hold the compass out in a *level position* directly in front of you; be *sure* it is level; then decide to go north. Consult the compass and ascertain in which direction the north lies. The compass needle points directly north with the north end of the needle; this end is usually black, sometimes pearl. Let your eye follow straight along the line pointed out by the needle; as you look ahead select a landmark—tree, rock, pond, or whatever may lie in that direction. Choose an object quite a distance off on the imaginary line, go directly toward it, and when intervening objects obscure the landmark, refer to your compass. If you have turned from the pathway north, face around and readjust your steps in the right direction. Do not let over two minutes pass without making sure by the compass that you are going on the right path, going directly north.

Common Compass.

Practise using the compass for a guide until you understand it; have faith in it and you may fearlessly trust to its guidance. Try going according to various points of the compass: suppose you wish to go southeast, the compass tells you this as plainly as the north; try it. Naturally, if you go to the southeast away from camp, return ing will be in exactly the opposite direction, and coming back to camp you must walk northwest. After learning to go in a straight line, guided entirely by the compass, try a zigzag path. A group of girls will find it good sport to practise trailing with the compass, and they will at the same time learn how to avoid being lost and how to help others find their way. It is possible to

Make a Compass of Your Watch
Besides keeping you company with its friendly nearness, its ticking and its ready answers to your questions regarding the time, a watch in the woods and fields has another use, for it can be used as a compass. It will show just where the south is, then by turning your back on the south you face the north, and on your right is the east and on your left the west. These are the rules:
With your watch in a horizontal position point the hour-hand to the sun, and if before noon, half-way between the hour hand and 12 is due south. If it is afternoon calculate the opposite way. For instance, if at 8 a. m. you point the hour-hand to the sun, 10 will point to the south, for that is half-way between 8 and 12. If at 2 p. m. you point the hour-hand to the sun, look back to 12, and half the distance will be at 1, therefore 1 points to the south.
An easy way to get the direction of the sun without looking directly at it is by means of the shadow of a straight, slender stick or grass stem thrown on the horizontal face of your watch. Hold the stick upright with the lower end touching the watch at the *point* of the hour-hand, then turn the watch until the shadow of the stick falls along the hour-hand. This will point the hand undeviatingly toward the sun.

Mountain Climbing
The campers should go together to climb the mountain, never one girl alone.
Before starting, find a strong stick to use as a staff; stow away some luncheon in one of your pockets; see that your camera is in perfect order, ready to use at a moment's notice; that your water-proof match-box is in your pocket filled with safety matches, your pocket-knife safe with you, also watch and compass, and that the tin cup is on your belt. Your whistle being always hung around your neck will, of course, be there as usual.
When you are ready, stand still and look about you once more to make sure of your bearings; close your eyes and tell yourself exactly what you have seen. After leaving camp and arriving at the foot of the mountain, take your bearings anew; then look up ahead and select a certain spot which you wish to reach on the upward trail. Having this definite object in view will help in making better progress and save your walking around in a circle, which is always the tendency when in a strange place and intervening trees or elevations obstruct the view, or when not sure of the way and trying to find it.
Begin blazing the trail at your first step up the mountain side. Even though there may be a trail already, you cannot be sure that it will continue; it is much safer to depend upon your own blazing.
Often in trailing along the mountain you will find huge rocks and steep depressions, or small lakes which you cannot cross over but must go around, and in so doing change your direction, perhaps strike off at an angle. Before making the detour, search out some large landmark, readily recognized after reaching the other side of the obstruction, a tall, peculiarly shaped tree or other natural feature. Now is the time to try earnestly to keep the landmark in sight as long as possible and to be able to recognize it when you see it again. Watch your compass and the sun that you may continue in the right direction after circling the obstruction. Go slow in climbing, take your time and don't get out of breath.
On many mountains the possibility of unexpected fogs exists, and safety requires that the party be linked together with a soft rope; the same precaution should be taken when the trail is very rough, steep, and rocky. The camper at the head of the line should tie the rope in a bow-line around her waist, with knot on left side, and eight or ten feet from her the next girl should link herself to the rope in the same manner; then another girl, and another, until the entire party is on the rope.
The leader starts on the trail and the others, holding fast to their staffs, carefully follow, each one cautious to keep the rope stretching out in front of her rather taut; then if one girl stumbles the others brace themselves and keep her from falling.
When descending the mountain, be careful to get a firm footing. Instead of facing the trail, it is safer to turn sideways, so that you can place the entire foot down and not risk the toes only, or the heels. Often coming down either a steep hill or a mountain is more difficult than going up.

Lost in the Woods
It is not at all probable that you will lose your way while on the trail, but if you should find yourself lost in the woods or in the open, the first thing to do is to remember that a brave girl does not get into a panic and so rob herself of judgment and the power to think clearly and act quickly. Believe firmly that you are *safe*, then sit down quietly and think out a plan of finding your way. Try to remember from which direction you have come and to recall landmarks. If you cannot do this, do not be frightened and do not allow any thought of possible harm to get a foothold in your mind. If there is a hill near, from which you can see any distance, climb that and get an outlook. You may be able to see the smoke of your camp-fire, which, after all, cannot be so far away. You may find a landmark that you do remember. If you see nothing which you can recognize, make a signal flag of your handkerchief and put it up high, as high as you can. Your friends will be looking for that. Then give the lost signal, one long blast with your whistle, and after a short pause follow

with two more blasts in quick succession. If you have no whistle shout, loud and long, then wait a while, keeping eyes and ears open to see and hear answering signals. If there is none, again shout the lost signal and continue the calls every little while for quite a time. Another call for help is the ascending smoke of three fires. This, of course, is for daylight. Build your fires some distance apart, twenty-five feet or more, that the smoke from each may be clearly seen alone, not mingled with the rest. Aim to create *smoke* rather than flame; a slender column of smoke can be seen a long distance, therefore the fire need not be large. Choose for your fires as clear a space and as high an elevation as can be found, and in the relief and excitement of rescue *do not forget to extinguish every spark* before leaving the ground.

If you decide to keep moving, blaze your trail as you go, so that it may be followed and also that you may know if you cross it again yourself. You can blaze the trail by breaking or bending small branches on trees and bushes, or by small strips torn from your handkerchief and tied conspicuously on twigs. If you are where there are no trees or undergrowth, build small piles of stones or little hills of earth at intervals to mark your trail.

If night overtakes you, look for the *North Star*. That will help if you know at what point of the compass your camp lies, and if you remember whether your course in leaving camp was to the north, south, east, or west, you can calculate pretty accurately whether the camp is to the north, south, east, or west of you.

In case the night must be spent where you are, go about making a shelter, prepare as comfortable a bed as possible, and do *not* be afraid. You will probably be found before morning, and you must be found in good physical condition.

If you can kindle a fire, do it; that will help to guide your friends and will ward off wild creatures that might startle you. Keep your fire going all night and take care that it does not spread.

It is better to remain quietly in one spot all night than to wander about in the dark and perhaps stumble upon dangerous places. If, when you find the points of the compass by the *North Star*, you mark them plainly on a stone or fallen log, they will be a ready guide for you as soon as daylight breaks.

The last word on this subject is: *Do not be afraid.*

To Find Your Way by the North Star

At night you will have the same reliable guide that has ever been the mariner's friend, and if you do not know this star guide, lose no time in finding it.

Polaris or pole-star is known generally as North Star, and this star is most important to the outdoor girl. At all times the North Star marks the north, its position never changes, and seeing that star and *knowing it*, you will always know the points of the compass. Face the North Star and you face the north. At your right hand is the east, at your left hand is the west, and at your back is the south.

Big Dipper.   *Little Dipper.*

NORTH STAR

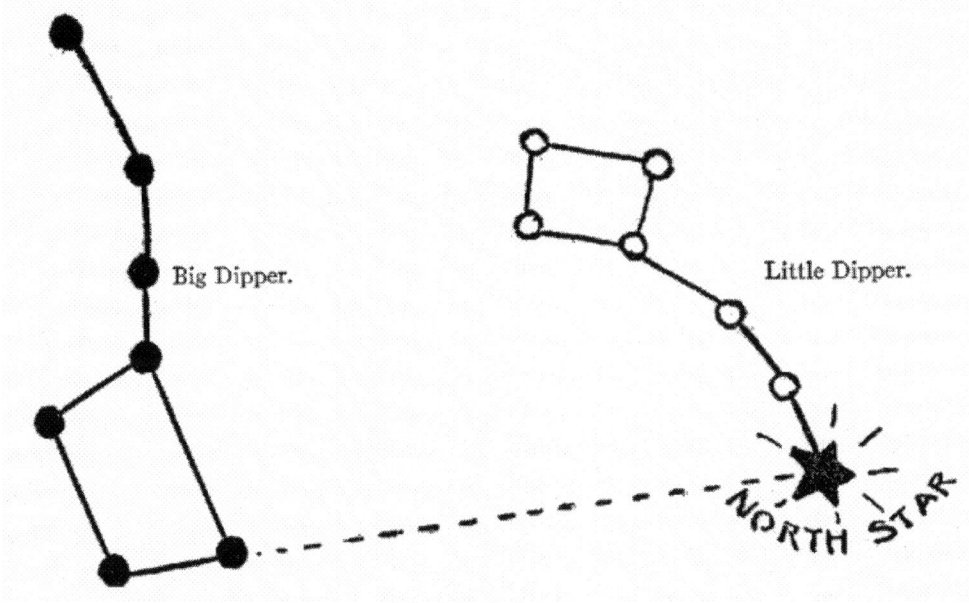

The North Star.

The North Star does not look very important because it is not very bright or very large, and were it not for the help of the Big Dipper, which every one knows, the North Star would not be easy to find. The diagram given on page 37 shows the relative position of the stars and will help you to find the North Star. The two stars forming the front side of the bowl of the Great Dipper point almost in a direct line to the North Star, which is the last one in the handle of the Little Dipper, or the tail of the Little Bear, which means the same thing.

CHAPTER III
CAMPING
Camp Sites. Water. Wood. Tents. Shelters. Lean-Tos. Fires. Cooking. Safety and Protection. Sanitation. Camp Spirit.

Information

Whether your camp is to be for one day, one week, or a longer period of time, the first question to be decided is: "Where shall we go?" If you know of no suitable spot, inquire of friends, and even if they have not personally enjoyed the delights of camping and sleeping in the open, one or more of them will probably know of some acquaintance who will be glad to give the information. Write to the various newspapers, magazines, railroads, and outdoor societies for suggestions. The Geological Survey of the United States at Washington, D. C., will furnish maps giving location and extent of forests and water-ways, also location and character of roads; you can obtain the maps for almost any part of every State. Most public automobile houses supply maps of any desired region. Send letters of inquiry to these sources of information, and in this way you will probably learn of many "just the right place" localities. Select a number of desirable addresses, investigate them, and make your own choice of location, remembering that the first three essentials for a camp are good ground, water, and wood; the rest is easy, for these three form the foundation for camping.

Location

Wherever you go, choose a dry spot, preferably in an open space near wooded land. Avoid hollows where the water will run into your shelters in wet weather; let your camp be so located that in case of rain the water will drain down away from it. Remember this or you may find your camp afloat upon a temporary lake or swamp should a storm arise.

Water

Pure drinking water you *must* have, it is of *vital* importance, so be sure to pitch your camp within near walking distance of a good spring, a securely covered well, or other supply of pure water.

Henry David Thoreau's method of obtaining clear water from a pond whose surface was covered with leaves, etc., was to push his pail, without tipping it in the least, straight down under the water until the top edge was below the surface several inches, then quickly lift it out; in doing this the overflow would carry off all leaves and twigs, leaving the remaining water in the pail clear and good. But you must first be sure that the pond contains pure water under the floating débris.

Always be cautious about drinking water from rivers, streams, ponds, and lakes though they may appear ever so clear and tempting, for the purity is by no means assured, and to drink from these sources may cause serious illness. Unless you are absolutely sure that water is free from impurities, *boil it*; then it will be safe to use for drinking and cooking.

Next in importance to good water is good fire-wood and woodsy material for shelters and beds. Bear this in mind when deciding upon the site for your camp.

Companions

Because your companions can make or mar the happiness in camp, it is safer to have in your party only those girls who will take kindly to the camp spirit of friendly helpfulness, those always ready to laugh and treat discomforts as jokes. This means that though fun-loving and full of buoyancy and life, each girl will willingly do her part and assume her share of responsibilities.

Safeguarding

You should also count among your companions two or more camp directors—possibly mothers of the girls, teachers, or older friends of whom the parents approve—who will enter heartily into all phases of outdoor life and while really being one with you in sport and work, will at the same time keep careful oversight and assure protection.

Avoid localities where there is a possibility of tramps or undesirable characters of any description, and do not wander from camp alone or unaccompanied by one of the directors. If your camp is in the forest it will be the part of wisdom to secure also a reliable guide who knows the forest ways.

The Start

The day before you leave for your camping-ground, have everything in readiness that there may be no delay when it is time to go. Be prompt, for you want to play fair and not keep the other girls waiting, causing them to lose valuable time.

The stimulating exhilaration which comes with trailing through the forests to camp, the keen delight of adventure, the charm of the wilderness, the freedom and wonder of living in the woods, all make for the health and happiness of the girl camper, and once experienced, ever after with the advent of spring comes the call of the untrammelled life in the big outdoors.

The One-Day Camp

Even a one-day camp fills the hours with more genuine lasting enjoyment than girls can find in other ways; there is a charm about it which clings in your memory, making a joy, later, of the mere thought and telling of the event.

That every moment of the day may be filled full of enjoyment for all, have a good programme, some definite, well-thought-out plan of activities and sports previously prepared, and if possible let every girl know beforehand just what she is to do when all arrive at camp.

With an older person in charge, the party could be divided, according to its size, into different groups, and as soon as the grounds are reached the groups should begin the fun of preparing for the camp dinner.

If the party consists of eight, two can gather fire-wood, two build the fireplace, two unpack the outfits, placing the provisions and cooking utensils in order conveniently near the fire, and two can bring the drinking water and cooking water.

Provisions and cooking utensils should be divided into as many packs as there are campers, and every camper carry a pack. Count in the outfit for each one a tin cup, preferably with open handle for wearing over belt.

In the one-day camp very few cooking utensils are needed; they may consist of two tin pails, one for drinking water, the other for boiling water, one coffee-pot for cocoa, one frying-pan for flapjacks or eggs, one large kitchen knife for general use, and one large spoon for stirring batter and cocoa.

Camp Dinner

Counting on a keen outdoor appetite for wholesome substantials, the provision list includes only plain fare, such as: Lamb chops, or thinly sliced bacon packed in oil-paper. Dry cocoa to which sugar has been added, carried in can or stout paper bag. One can of condensed milk, unsweetened, to be diluted with water according to directions on can. Butter in baking-powder can. Dry flour mixed with salt and baking-powder in required proportions for flapjacks, packed in strong paper bag and carried in one of the tin pails. Bread in loaf wrapped in wax-paper. Potatoes washed and dried ready to cook, packed in paper bag or carried in second tin pail. Pepper and salt each sealed in separate marked envelopes; when needed, perforate paper with big pin and use envelopes as shakers. One egg for batter, buried in the flour to prevent breaking, and one small can of creamy maple sugar, soft enough to spread on hot cakes, or a can of ordinary maple syrup.

The Clean-Up

While resting after dinner is the time for story-telling; then, before taking part in sports of any kind, every particle of débris, even small bits of egg-shell and paper, should be gathered up and burned until not a vestige remains. To be "good sports," thought must be taken for the next comers and the camping-ground left in perfect order, absolutely free from litter or débris of any kind.

When breaking camp be *sure* to soak the fire with water again and again. It is criminal to leave any coals or even a spark of the fire smouldering.

Be *positive* that the *fire is out*.

A permanent camp.

Shelters and Tents. Lean-To

For a fixed camp of longer or shorter duration your home will be under the shelter of boughs, logs, or canvas. The home of green boughs is considered by many the ideal of camp shelters. This you can make for yourself. It is a simple little two-sided, slanting roof and back and open-front shed, made of the material of the woods and generally known as a lean-to, sometimes as Baker tent when of canvas.

There are three ways of erecting the front framework.

Outdoor shelters.

The first is to find two trees standing about seven feet apart with convenient branches down low enough to support the horizontal top cross pole when laid in the crotches. Lacking the proper trees, the second method is to get two strong, straight, forked poles of green wood and drive them down into the ground deep enough to make them stand firm and upright by themselves the required distance apart. The third way is to reinforce the uprights by shorter forked stakes driven firmly into the ground and braced against the uprights, but this is not often necessary.

Having your uprights in place, extending above ground five feet or more, lay a top pole across, fitting its ends into the forked tops of the uprights. Against this top pole rest five or six slender poles at regular distances apart, one end of each against the top pole and the other end on the ground slanting outward and backward sufficiently to give a good slope and allow sleeping space beneath. At right angles to the slanting poles, lay across them other poles, using the natural pegs or stumps left on the slanting poles by lopped-off branches, as braces to hold the cross poles in place (Fig. 18).

When building the frame be sure to place the slanting poles so that the little stumps left on them will turn *up* and not down, that they may hold the cross poles. Try to have spaces between cross poles as regular as possible. A log may be rolled up against the ground ends of the slanting poles to prevent their slipping, though this is rarely necessary, for they stand firm as a rule.

You can cover the frame with bark and then thatch it, which will render the shelter better able to withstand a storm, or you may omit the bark, using only the thatch as a covering. Put on very thick, this should make the lean-to rain-proof.

With small tips of branches from trees, preferably balsam, hemlock, or other evergreens, begin thatching your shelter. Commence at the bottom of the lean-to, and hook on the thatch branches close together all the way across the lowest cross pole, using the stumps of these thatch branches as hooks to hold the thatch in place on the cross pole (Fig. 19). Overlap the lower thatches as you work along the next higher cross pole, like shingles on a house, and continue in this way, overlapping each succeeding cross pole with an upper row of thatch until the top is reached. Fill in the sides thick with branches, boughs, or even small, thick trees.

The lean-to frame can be covered with your poncho in case of necessity, but boughs are much better.

Permanent Camp. Lean-To. Open Camp

Another kind of lean-to intended for a permanent camp is in general use throughout the Adirondacks. It is built of substantial good-sized logs put together log-cabin fashion, with open front, slanting roof, and low back (Fig. 20). This shelter has usually a board floor raised a few inches above the ground and covered thick, at least a foot deep, with balsam. Overspread with blankets, the soft floor forms a comfortable bed. A log across the front of the floor keeps the balsam in place and forms a seat for the campers in the evenings when gathered for a social time before the fire. The roof of the log lean-to can be either of boards or well-thatched poles which have first been overlaid with bark.

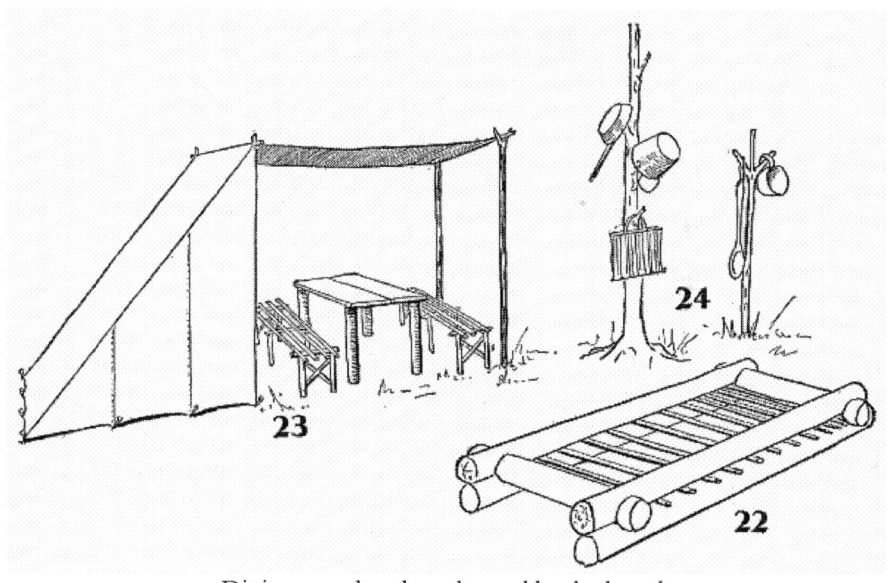

Dining-tent, handy racks, and log bedstead.

One of the most comfortable and delightful of real forest camps which I have ever been in, was a permanent camp in the Adirondacks owned and run by one of the best of Adirondack guides. The camp consisted of several shelters and two big permanent fireplaces.

Over the ground space for the large tent outlined with logs was a strong substantial rustic frame, built of material at hand in the forest and intended to last many seasons (Fig. 21). The shelter boasted of two springy, woodsy beds, made of slender logs laid crosswise and raised some inches from the ground. These slender logs slanted down slightly from head to foot of the bed, and the edges of the bed were built high enough to hold the deep thick filling of balsam tips, so generously deep as to do away with all consciousness of the underlying slender-log foundation (Fig. 22). Each bed was wide enough for two girls and the shelter ample to accommodate comfortably four campers. There could have been one more bed, when the tent would have sheltered six girls.

In the late fall, the guide removed the water-proof tent covering and kept it in a safe, dry place until needed, leaving the beds and bare tent frame standing.

There was a smaller tent and also a lean-to in this camp.

A forest camp by the water.

The dining-table, contrived of logs and boards, was sheltered by a square of canvas on a rustic frame (Fig. 23). The camp dishes of white enamel ware were kept in a wooden box, nailed to a close-by tree; in this box the guide had put shelves, resting them on wooden cleats. The cupboard had a door that shut tight and fastened securely to keep out the little wild creatures of the woods. Pots, kettles, frying-pan, etc., hung on the stubs of a slender tree where branches and top had been lopped off (Fig. 24). The sealed foods were stowed away in a box cupboard, and canned goods were cached in a cave-like spot under a huge rock, with opening secured by stones. The walls of the substantial fireplace, fully two feet high, were of big stones, the centre filled in part-way with earth, and the cook-fire was made on top of the earth, so there was not the slightest danger of the fire spreading.

The soft, warm, cheerful-colored camp blankets when not in use were stored carefully under cover of a water-proof tent-like storehouse, with the canvas sides dropped from the ridge-pole, both sides and flaps securely fastened and the entire storehouse made proof against intrusion.

This camp was located near a lake in the mountain forest and its charm was indescribably delightful.

Tents

Tents in almost endless variety of shapes and sizes are manufactured and sold by camp-outfitters and sporting-goods shops. The tents range from small canoe-tents, accommodating one person only, to the large wall-tents for four or more people. When using tents, difficulties of transportation and extra weight can be overcome by having tent poles and pegs cut in the forest.

If you purchase tents, full instructions for erection go with them. Write for illustrated catalogues to various outfitters and look the books over carefully before buying. Your choice will depend upon your party, length of stay, and location of camp.

You may be able to secure a discarded army-tent that has never been used, is in good condition, and has been condemned merely for some unimportant blemish.

Such tents are very serviceable and can be purchased at Government auctions, or from dealers who themselves have bought them from the Government.

In camp.

A large square seven by seven feet, or more, of balloon silk, water-proof cloth, or even heavy unbleached sheeting, will be found most useful in camp. Sew strong tape strings at the four corners and at intervals along the sides for tying to shelters, etc. The water-proof cloth will serve as a drop-curtain in front of the lean-to during a hard storm, or as carpet cloth over ground of shelter, also as an extra shelter, either lean-to or tent style; any of the three materials can do duty as windbreak, fly to shelter, or dining canopy, and may be used in other ways.

Camp-Beds

To derive joy and strength from your outing it is of serious importance that you sleep well every night while at camp, and your camp-bed must be comfortable to insure a good night's rest.

A bough-bed is one of the joys of the forest when it is *well made*, and to put it together properly will require about half an hour's time, but the delight of sleeping on a soft balsam bed perfumed with the pungent odors of the balsam will well repay for the time expended.

The bough-bed, the cook-fire, and the wall-tent.

Bough-Bed

Tips of balsam broken off with your fingers about fourteen inches long make the best of beds, but hemlock, spruce, and other evergreens can be used; if they are not obtainable, the fan-like branches from other trees may take their place. Of these you will need a large quantity, in order to have the bed springy and soft. Always place the outdoor bed with the head well under cover and foot toward the opening of shelter, or if without shelter, toward the fire. Make the bed by arranging the branches shingle-like in *very* thick overlapping rows, convex side up, directly on the ground with *thick end* of stems *toward* the *foot*. Push these ends into the ground so that the tips will be raised slantingly up from the earth; make the rows which will come under the hips extra thick and springy. Continue placing the layers in this manner until the space for single or double bed, as the case may be, is covered with the first layer of your green mattress. Over it make another layer of branches, reversing the ends of these tips from those underneath by pushing the *thick ends* of branches of this top layer slantingly into the under layer *toward* the *head* of the bed with tips toward the foot. Make more layers, until the bed is about two feet thick (Fig. 25); then cover the mattress thus made with your poncho, rubber side down, and on top spread one of the sleeping blankets, using the other one as a cover. Be sure to allow plenty of time for this work and have the bed dry and soft.

Bag-Bed

When the camp is located where there is no material for a bough-bed, each girl can carry with her a bag three feet wide and six and one-half feet long, made of strong cloth, ticking, soft khaki, or like material, to be filled with leaves, grass, or other browse found on or near the camp-grounds. Such a mattress made up with poncho and blankets is very satisfactory, but it must be well filled, so that when you lie on the mattress it will not mash flat and hard.

Cot-Bed

For an entire summer camp army cots which fold for packing are good and very comfortable with a doubled, thick quilt placed on top for a mattress.

The sporting-goods stores show a great variety of other beds, cots, and sleeping-bags, and a line to them will bring illustrated catalogues, or, if in the city, you can call and see the goods. Any of the beds I have described, however, can be used to advantage, and I heartily endorse the *well-made* bough-bed, especially if of balsam.

Pillows

Make a bag one-half yard square of brown linen or cotton cloth, and when you reach camp, gather the best browse you can find for filling, but be careful about having the pillow too full; keep it soft and comfortable. If there is no browse, use clean underwear in its place. Fasten the open end of the bag together with large-sized patent dress snappers.

One of the pleasantest phases of a season's camping are the little side trips for overnight. You hit the trail that leads to the chosen spot located some two or three, perhaps six or seven, miles distant; a place absolutely dry, where you can enjoy the fun of sleeping on the ground without shelter, having merely the starry sky for a canopy. Each girl can select the spot where she is to sleep and free it from all twigs, stones, etc., as the smallest and most insignificant of these will rob her of sleep and make the night most uncomfortable. When the space is smooth mark the spot where the shoulders rest when lying down and another spot immediately under the hips, then dig a hollow for each to fit in easily; cover the sleeping space with poncho, rubber side down, and over this lay a folded blanket for a mattress, using the second blanket as a cover. Your sleep will then probably be sound and refreshing.

Guards

Establish watchers, for this temporary camp, in relays to keep guard through the night and care for the fire, not allowing it to spread, grow too hot, or die down and go out.

If there are eight in the party, the first two, starting in at 10 p. m., will keep vigil until 12 midnight. These may chance to see a porcupine or other small wild animal, but the little creatures will not come too near as long as your camp-fire is burning. The next two watchers will be on duty until 2 a. m., and will doubtless hear, if not see, some of the wild life of the forest. The third couple's turn lasts until 4 a. m.; then the last two will be awakened in time to see the sun rise, listen to the twittering and singing of the wild birds, and possibly catch a glimpse of wild deer. With 6 a. m. comes broad daylight, and the ever-to-be-remembered night in the open is past and gone.

These side trips bring you into closer touch with nature, quicken your love for, and a desire to know more of, the wild; and, much to the delight of the campers keeping guard through the hours of the night, there comes a keen sense of the unusual, of novel experience, of strangeness and adventure.

Soft wood.

Exercise
While wholesome camping calls for sufficient physical exercise to cause a girl to be blissfully tired at night, and yet awaken refreshed and full of energy the next morn ing with a good appetite for breakfast, until you become accustomed to the outdoor life, it is best to curb your ambition to outdo the other girls in strength and endurance. It is best not to overtax yourself by travelling too far on a long trail at one stretch, or by lifting too heavy a log, stone, or other weight.

The Camp-Fire
The outdoor fire in camp bespeaks cheer, comfort, and possibilities for a hot dinner, all of which the camper appreciates.

How to Build a Fire

Choose an open space, if possible, for your fire. Beware of having it under tree branches, too near a tent, or in any other place that might prove dangerous. Start your fire with the tinder nearest at hand, dry leaves, ferns, twigs, cones, birch bark, or pine-knot slivers. As the tinder begins to burn, add kindling-wood of larger size, always remembering that the air must circulate under and upward through the kindling; no fire can live without air any more than you can live without breathing. Smother a person and he will die, smother a fire and it will die.

Hard wood.

Soft woods are best to use after lighting the tinder; they ignite easily and burn quickly, such as pine, spruce, alder, birch, soft maple, balsam-fir, and others. When the kindling is blazing put on still heavier wood, until you have a good, steady fire. Hard wood is better than soft when the fire is well going; it burns longer and can usually be depended upon for a reliable fire, not sending out sparks or sputtering, as do many of the soft woods, but burning well and giving a fine bed of hot coals. The tree belonging exclusively to America, and which is the best of the hardwoods, comes first on the hardwood list. This is *hickory*. Pecan, chestnut-oak, black birch, basket-oaks, white birch, maple, dogwood, beech, red and yellow birch, ash, and apple wood when obtainable are excellent.

Cook-Fire

Make the cook-fire *small* and *hot*; then you can work over it in comfort and not scorch both hands and face when trying to get near enough to cook, as would be the case if the fire were large.
When in a hurry use dry bark as wood for the cook-fire. Hemlock, pine, hickory, and other bark make a hot fire in a short time, and water will boil quickly over a bark fire.

Log-Cabin Fire

Start this fire with two good-sized short sticks or logs. Place them about one foot apart parallel to each other. At each end across these lay two smaller sticks, and in the hollow square formed by the four sticks, put the tinder of cones, birch bark, or dry leaves.

Across the two upper sticks and over the tinder, make a grate by laying slender kindling sticks across from and resting on top of the two upper large sticks. Over the grate, at right angles to the sticks forming it, place more sticks of larger size. Continue in this way, building the log-cabin fire until the structure is one foot or so high, each layer being placed at right angles to the one beneath it. The fire must be lighted from beneath in the pile of tinder. I learned this method when on the Pacific slope. The fire burns quickly, and the log-cabin plan is a good one to follow when heating the bean hole, as the fire can be built over the hole, and in burning the red-hot coals will fall down into it, or the fire can be built directly in the hole; both ways are used by campers.

Fire in the Rain
To build a fire in the rain with no dry wood in sight seems a difficult problem, but keep cheerful, hum your favorite tune, and look for a pine-knot or birch bark and an old dead stump or log. In the centre of the dead wood you will find dry wood; dig it out and, after starting the fire with either birch bark or pine-knot, use the dry wood as kindling. When it begins to burn, add larger pieces of wood, and soon the fire will grow strong enough to burn wet wood. If there happens to be a big rock in your camp, build your fire on the sheltered side and directly against the stone, which will act as a windbreak and keep the driving rain from extinguishing the fire. A slightly shelving bank would also form a shelter for it. A pine-knot is always a good friend to the girl camper, both in dry and wet weather, but is especially friendly when it rains and everything is dripping wet.
You will find pine-knots in wooded sections where pine-trees grow; or, if you are located near water where there are no trees, look for pine knots in driftwood washed ashore. When secured cut thin slices down part way all around the elongated knot and circle it with many layers of shavings until the knot somewhat resembles a toy tree. The inside will be absolutely dry, and this branching knot will prove reliable and start your fire without fail. Birch bark will start a fire even when the bark is damp, and it is one of the best things you can have as a starter for an outdoor, rainy-day fire.
Take your cue from the forest guides, and while in the woods always carry some dry birch bark in your pocket for a fire in case of rain.

Camp Fireplace
One way to make the outdoor fireplace is to lay two *green* logs side by side on the ground in a narrow V shape, but open at both ends; only a few inches at one end, a foot or more at the other. The fire is built between the logs, and the frying-pan and pail of water, resting on both logs, bridge across the fire. Should the widest space between the logs be needed, place two slender green logs at right angles across the V logs, and have these short top cross logs near enough together to hold the frying-pans set on them (Fig. 26).
When there are no green logs, build the fireplace with three rectangular sides of stone, open front, and make the fire in the centre; the pots and pans rest across the fire on the stones.
If neither stones nor logs are available, dig a circle of fresh earth as a safeguard and have the fire in its centre. Here you will need two strong, forked-top stakes driven down into the ground directly opposite each other, one on each side of the circle. Rest the end of a stout green stick in the forked tops of the stakes, and use it to hang pots and pails from when cooking. A fire can also be safeguarded with a circle of stones placed close together. Another method of outdoor cooking may be seen on page 81, where leaning stakes are used from which to hang cooking utensils over the fire.
One more caution about possibilities of causing forest fire. Terrible wide-spread fires have resulted from what was supposed to be an extinguished outdoor fire. Do not trust it, but when you are sure the camp-fire is out, pour on more water over the fire and all around the unburned edge of surrounding ground; then throw on fresh earth until the fire space is

covered. Be always on the safe side. Tack up on a tree in the camp, where all must see it, a copy of the state laws regarding forest fires, as shown in photograph frontispiece.

Bringing wood for the fire.

On forest lands much of the ground is deep with tangled rootlets and fibres mixed in with the mould, and a fire may be smouldering down underneath, where you cannot see it. *Have a care.*

The permanent-camp fireplace, built to do service for several seasons, is usually of big, heavy, *green* logs, stones, and earth. The logs, about three and one-half feet long, are built log-cabin fashion, some twenty-eight inches high, with all crevices filled in and firmly padded with earth and stones. Big stones are anchored securely along the top of the earth-covered log sides and back of the fireplace, raising these higher than the front. The space inside the walled fireplace is very nearly filled up with earth, and the fire is built on this earth. Surfaces of logs which may have been left exposed where the fire is to be made are safeguarded with earth (Fig. 27).

Such a fireplace is big, substantial, firm, and lasting. Many of them may be seen in the Adirondacks. They usually face the camp shelter, but are located at a safe distance, fully two yards, from it. Fires built in these are generally used as social cheer-fires, but you can have the cheer-fire even though the substantial fireplace be *non est*, if in the evening you pile more wood on the cook-fire, making it large enough for all to gather around and have a good time, telling stories, laughing, talking, and singing.

An excellent rule in camp is to have always on hand *plenty* of *fire-wood*. Replenish the reserve stock every day as inroads are made upon it, and have some sort of shelter or covering where the wood will be kept dry and ready for immediate use.

Camp Cooking. Provisions

In the woods one is generally hungry except immediately after a good meal, and provisions and cooking are of vital interest to the camper. The list of essentials is not very long and, when the camp is a permanent one, non-essentials may be added to the larder with advantage.

Bread of some kind will form part of every meal, and a few loaves freshly baked can be taken to camp to start with while you are getting settled.

The quickest bread to cook is the delectable flapjack, and it is quite exciting to toss it in the air, see it turn over and catch it again—if you can.

Flapjacks

Mix dry flour, baking-powder, and salt together, 1 good teaspoonful of Royal baking-powder to every 2 cups of flour, and 1 level teaspoonful of salt to 1 quart (4 cups) of flour. To make the batter, beat 1 egg and add 1½ cups of milk, or 1 cup of milk and ½ cup of water; unsweetened condensed milk diluted according to directions on can may be used. Carefully and gradually stir in enough of the flour you have prepared to make a creamy batter, be sure it is smooth and without lumps; then stir in 1 heaping teaspoonful of sugar, better still molasses, to make the cakes brown. Grease the frying-pan with a piece of fat pork or bacon, have the pan hot, and, with a large spoon or a cup, ladle out the batter into the pan, forming three small cakes to be turned by a knife, or one large cake to be turned by tossing. Use the knife to lift the edges of the cakes as they cook, and when you see them a golden brown, turn quickly. Or, if the cake is large, loosen it; then lift the pan and quickly toss the cake up into the air in such a way that it will turn over and land safely, brown side up, on the pan. Unless you are skilled in tossing flapjacks, don't risk wasting the cake by having it fall on the ground or in the fire, but confine your efforts to the small, knife-turned cakes. Serve them "piping hot," and if there are no plates, each camper can deftly and quickly roll her flapjack into cylinder form of many layers and daintily and comfortably eat it while holding the roll between forefinger and thumb.

Keep the frying-pan well greased while cooking the cakes, rubbing the pan with grease each time before pouring in fresh batter.

Flapjacks are good with butter, delicious with creamy maple-sugar soft enough to spread smoothly over the butter. The sugar comes in cans. Ordinary maple-syrup can be used, but is apt to drip over the edges if the cake is held in the hand.

Well-cooked cold rice mixed with the batter will give a delicate griddle-cake and make a change from the regular flapjack.

Biscuits

Biscuits are more easily made than raised bread and so are used largely in its place while in camp. The proportions of flour and baking-powder are the same as for flapjacks. To 4 cups of flour mix 2 teaspoonfuls of Royal baking-powder and 1 level teaspoonful of salt; add shortening about the size of an egg, either lard or drippings. Divide the shortening into small bits and, using the tips of your fingers, rub it well into the dry flour just prepared;

then gradually stir in cold water to make a soft dough, barely stiff enough to be rolled out ¾ inch thick on bread-board, clean flat stone, or large, smooth piece of flattened bark. Whichever is used must be well floured, as must also the rolling-pin and biscuit cutter. A clean glass bottle or smooth round stick may be used as rolling-pin, and the cutter can be a baking-powder can, or the biscuits may be cut square, or 4 inches long and 2 inches wide with a knife. The dough may also be shaped into a loaf ¾ inch thick and baked in a pan by planting the pan in a bed of hot coals, covering it with another pan or some substitute, and placing a deep layer of hot coals all over the cover. The biscuits should bake in about fifteen minutes. For a hurry meal each camper can take a strip of dough, wind it spirally around a peeled thick stick, which has first been heated, and cook her own spiral biscuit by holding it over the fire and constantly turning the stick. Biscuits, in common with everything cooked over a hot wood-fire, need constant watching that they may not burn. Test them with a clean splinter of wood; thrust it into the biscuit and if no dough clings to the wood the biscuits are done.

Johnny-Cake
Served hot, split open and buttered, these Kentucky johnny-cakes with a cup of good coffee make a fine, hearty breakfast, very satisfying and good.
Allow ½ cup of corn-meal for each person, and to every 4 cups of meal add 1 teaspoonful of salt, mix well; then pour water, which is *boiling hard*, gradually into the meal, stirring constantly to avoid having any lumps. When the consistency is like soft mush, have ready a frying-pan almost full of *hot* drippings or lard, dip your hands into cold water to enable you to handle the hot dough, and, taking up enough corn-meal dough to make a *large*-sized biscuit, pat it in your hands into a ¾-inch-thick cake and gently drop it into the hot fat; immediately make another cake, drop it into the fat, and continue until the frying-pan is full. As soon as one johnny-cake browns on the lower side turn it over, remove each cake from the fat as soon as done, and serve as they cook.
Corn-meal must be thoroughly scalded with boiling water when making any kind of corn bread in order to have the bread soft and not dry and "chaffy."
For baked corn bread add 2 full teaspoons of baking-powder and stir in 2 eggs, after 4 cups of meal and 1 teaspoonful of salt have been thoroughly scalded and allowed to cool a little. Pour this corn-meal dough into a pan which has been generously greased, and bake.
Corn-meal needs a hot oven and takes longer to bake than wheat-flour biscuits.

Corn-Meal Mush
Corn-meal mush does not absolutely require fresh cream or milk when served. It is good eaten with butter and very nourishing. Many like it with maple-syrup or common molasses.
Time is required to make well-cooked mush; at least one hour will be necessary. To 2 quarts of boiling, bubbling water add 1 teaspoonful of salt, and very slowly, little by little, add 2 cups of corn-meal, stirring constantly and not allowing the water to cease boiling. Do not stop stirring until the mush has cooked about ten minutes. It may then be placed higher up from the fire, where it will not scorch, and *boiling* water added from time to time as needed to keep the mush of right consistency. The cold mush may be made into a tempting dish, if sliced ½-inch thick and fried brown in pork fat. Many cold cooked cereals can be treated in the same way; sprinkled with flour these will brown better.

Kentucky Bread
Kentucky bread is made of flour, salt, and water. It is generally known as beaten biscuit. Mix 2 scant teaspoonfuls of salt with 1 quart of flour, add enough cold water to make a *stiff*, smooth dough and knead, pull, and pound the dough until it blisters; the longer it is worked and beaten the better. Roll out very thin, cut round or into squares and bake. These biscuits may be quickly made, are simple and wholesome.

Cocoa
Good cocoa may be made by substituting cold milk and cold water for hot. Follow directions on the can as to proportion, and add the cold liquids after the cocoa is mixed to a smooth paste; then boil. Either unsweetened condensed milk or milk powder can take the place of fresh milk.

Coffee
For every camper allow 1 tablespoonful of ground coffee, then 1 extra spoonful for the pot. Put the dry coffee into the coffee-pot, and to settle it add a crumbled egg-shell; then pour in a little cold water and stir all together; when there are no egg-shells use merely cold water. Add 1 cupful of cold water for each camper, and 2 for the pot, set the coffee-pot over the fire and let it boil for a few moments, take it from the fire and pour into the spout a little cold water, then place the coffee where it will keep hot—not cook, but settle.

Tea
Allow 1 scant teaspoonful of tea for each person, scald the teapot, measure the tea into the pot, and pour in as many cups of *boiling* water as there are spoonfuls of tea, adding an extra cupful for the pot. *Never let tea boil.*

Boiled Potatoes
Wash potatoes, cut out any blemish, and put them on to cook in cold water over the fire. They are much better boiled while wearing their jackets. Allow from one-half to three-quarters of an hour for boiling, test them with a sliver of wood that will pierce through the centre when the potato is done. When cooked pour off the boiling water, set off the fire to one side where they will keep hot, and raise one edge of the lid to allow the steam to escape. Serve while *very* hot.

Baked Potatoes
Wrap each potato in wet leaves and place them all on hot ashes that lie over hot coals, put more hot ashes on top of the potatoes, and over the ashes place a deep bed of red-hot coals. It will require about forty minutes or more for potatoes to bake. Take one out when you think they should be done; if soft enough to yield to the pressure when squeezed between thumb and finger, the potato is cooked. Choose potatoes as near of a size as possible; then all will be baked to a turn at the same time.

Bean Soup and Baked Beans
Look over one quart of dried beans, take out all bits of foreign matter and injured beans; then wash the beans in several waters and put them to soak overnight in fresh water. Next morning scald 1½ pounds salt pork, scrape it well, rinse, and with 1 teaspoonful of dried onion or half of a fresh one, put on to boil with the beans in cold water. Cook slowly for several hours. When the water boils low, add more boiling water and boil until the beans are soft.
To make soup, dip out a heaping cupful of the boiled beans, mash them to a paste, then pour the liquid from the boiled beans over the paste and stir until well mixed; if too thin add more beans; if too thick add hot water until of the right consistency, place the soup over the fire to reheat, and serve very hot. To bake beans, remove the pork from the drained, partially cooked beans, score it across the top and replace it in the pot in midst of and extending a trifle above the surface of the beans, add 1 cup of hot water and securely cover the top of the pot with a lid or some substitute. Sink the pot well into the glowing coals and shovel hot coals over all. Add more hot water from time to time if necessary.

Beans cooked in a bean hole rival those baked in other ways. Dig the hole about 1½ feet deep and wide, build a fire in it, and keep it burning briskly for hours; the oven hole must be *hot*. When the beans are ready, rake the fire out of the hole; then sink the pot down into the hole and cover well with hot coals and ashes, placing them all over the sides and top of the pot. Over these shovel a thick layer of earth, protecting the top with grass sod or thick blanket of leaves and bark, that rain may not penetrate to the oven. Let the beans bake all night.

Bacon
Sliced bacon freshly cut is best; do not bring it to camp in jars or cans, but cut it as needed. Each girl may have the fun of cooking her own bacon.
Cut long, slender sticks with pronged ends, sharpen the prongs and they will hold the bacon; or use sticks with split ends and wedge in the bacon between the two sides of the split, then toast it over the fire. Other small pieces of meat can be cooked in the same way. Bacon boiled with greens gives the vegetable a fine flavor, as it also does string-beans when cooked with them. It may, however, be boiled alone for dinner, and is good fried for breakfast.

Game Birds
Game birds can be baked in the embers. Have ready a bed of red-hot coals covered with a thin layer of ashes, and after drawing the bird, dip it in water to wet the feathers; then place it on the ash-covered red coals, cover the bird with more ashes, and heap on quantities of red coals. If the bird is small it should be baked in about one-half hour. When done strip off the skin, carrying feathers with it, and the bird will be clean and appetizing. Birds can also be roasted in the bean-pot hole, but in this way, they must first be picked, drawn, and rinsed clean; then cut into good-sized pieces and placed in the pot with fat pork, size of an egg, for seasoning; after pouring in enough water to cover the meat, fasten the pot lid on securely and bury the pot in the glowing hot hole under a heap of red-hot coals. Cover with earth, the same as when baking beans.

Fish
Fish cooked in the embers is very good, and you need not first remove scales or fins, but clean the fish, season it with salt and pepper, wrap it in fresh, wet, green leaves or wet blank paper, not printed paper, and bury in the coals the same as a bird. When done the skin, scales, and fins can all be pulled off together, leaving the delicious hot fish ready to serve.
To boil a fish: First scale and clean it; then cut off head and tail. If you have a piece of new cheesecloth to wrap the fish in, it can be stuffed with dressing made of dry crumbs of bread or biscuits well seasoned with butter, or bits of pork, pepper, and a very small piece of onion. The cloth covering must be wrapped around and tied with white string. When the fish is ready, put it into boiling water to which has been added 1 tablespoonful of vinegar and a little salt. The vinegar tends to keep the meat firm, and the dressing makes the fish more of a dinner dish; both, however, can be omitted. Allow about twenty minutes for boiling a three-pound fish.
The sooner a fish is cooked after being caught the better. To scale a fish, lay it on a flat stone or log, hold it by the head and with a knife scrape off the scales. Scale each side and, with a quick stroke, cut off the head and lower fins. The back fin must have incisions on each side in order to remove it. Trout are merely scraped and cleaned by drawing out the inside with head and gills. Do this by forcing your hand in and grasping tight hold of the gullet.
To clean most fish it is necessary to slit open the under side, take out the inside, wash the fish, and wipe it dry with a clean cloth.

If the camping party is fond of fish, and fish frequently forms part of a meal, have a special clean cloth to use exclusively for drying the fish.

Provisions for One Person for Two Weeks. To be Multiplied by Number of Campers, and Length of Time if Stay is over Two Weeks

Essential Foods

Outdoor life seems to require certain kinds of foods; these we call essentials; others in addition to them are in the nature of luxuries or non-essentials.

List

Essentials

Wheat flour	6		lbs.
Corn-meal	2	½	lbs.
Baking-powder		½	lb.
Coffee		½	lb.
Tea		1/8	lb.
Cocoa		½	lb.
Pork	1		lb.
Bacon	2	½	lbs.
Salt		½	lb.
Pepper	1		oz.
Sugar	3		lbs.
Butter	1	½	lbs.
Milk, dried		½	lb.
Lard		¾	lb.
Egg powder		¼	lb.
Fruit, dried	1		lb.
Potatoes, dried	1	½	lbs.
Beans	1	½	lbs.
Maple-syrup	1		pt.
Vinegar		¼	pt.

List

Non-Essentials

Rice	2	½	lbs.
Lemons		½	doz.
Erbswurst		¼	lb.
Soup tablets		¼	lb.
Baker's chocolate (slightly sweetened)		½	lb.
Maple-sugar		½	lb.
Ham	5		lbs.
Nuts	2		lbs.
Marmalade		½	jar
Preserves	1		can
Citric acid		1/8	lb.
Onions, dried	1		oz.
Cheese	1		lb.
Potatoes, fresh	14		
Codfish	1		lb.
Vegetables, dried		½	lb.

Sanitation

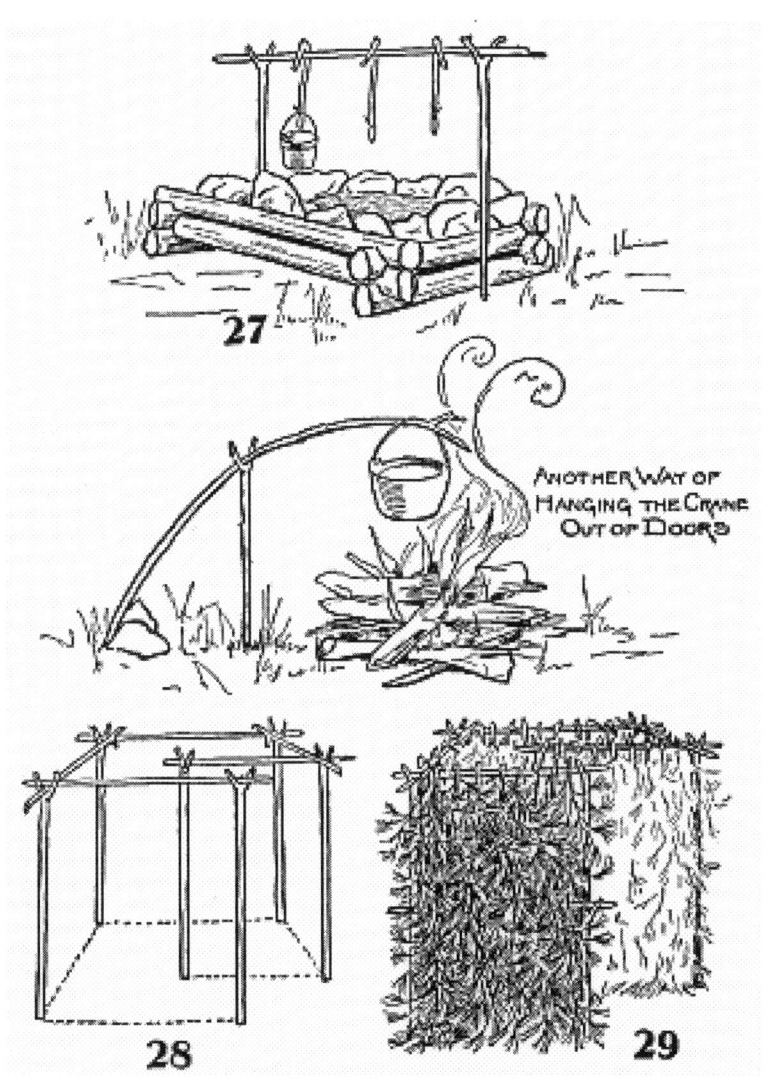

Camp fires and camp sanitation.

Keep your camp scrupulously clean. Do not litter up the place, your health and happiness greatly depend upon observing the laws of hygiene. Make sure after each meal that all kitchen refuse is collected and deposited in the big garbage hole, previously dug for that purpose, and well covered with a layer of fresh earth.

Impress upon your mind that fresh earth is a disinfectant and keeps down all odors.
Erect a framework with partially open side entrance for a retiring-room. Use six strong forked-topped poles planted in an irregular square as uprights (Fig. 28), and across these lay slender poles, fitting the ends well into the forked tops of the uprights (Fig. 28). Half-way down from the top, place more cross poles, resting them on the crotches left on the uprights. Have these last cross poles as nearly the same distance from the ground as possible and over them hang thick branches, hooking the branches on by the stubs on their heavy ends. Also hang thickly foliaged branches on the top cross poles, using the stubs

41

where smaller branches have been lopped off as hooks, as on the lower row (Fig. 29); then peg down the bottom ends of the hanging branches to the ground with sharpened two-pronged crotches cut from branches. The upper row of branches should overlap the under row one foot or more. Make the seat by driving three stout stakes firmly into the ground; two at the back, one in front, and on these nail three crosspieces.

Never throw dish water or any refuse near your tent or on the camp grounds.

Burn or *bury* all trash, remembering that earth and fire are your good servants, and with their assistance you can have perfect camp cleanliness, which will go a long way toward keeping away a variety of troublesome flies and make camp attractive and wholesome.

Camp Spirit

Thoughtfulness for others; kindliness; the willingness to do your share of the work, and more, too; the habit of making light of all discomforts; cheerfulness under all circumstances; and the determination never to sulk, imagine you are slighted, or find fault with people, conditions, or things. To radiate good-will, take things as they come and *enjoy them*, and to do your full share of entertainment and fun-making—this is the true camp spirit.

CHAPTER IV
WHAT TO WEAR ON THE TRAIL

Camp Outfits. Clothing. Personal Outfits. Camp Packs. Duffel-Bags and What to Put in Them

To prepare your own camping outfit for the coming summer, to plan, to work out your lists, to select materials, and make many of the things just as you want them or even to hunt up the articles and purchase them, while all the time delightful visions of trailing and camp life dance before you, is to know the true joy of anticipation, and is great fun.

Clothing

Make your dress for the trail absolutely comfortable, not too heavy, too tight, too hot, or too cool. No part of the clothing should bind or draw.

Brown or dark gray are the best colors for the forest; avoid wearing those which frighten the timid wild life, for you want to make friends with the birds and animals, so do not wear metal buttons, buckles, or anything that shines or sparkles.

Underwear

For girl campers the light-weight, pure-woollen underwear is best, especially if you locate in the mountains, or the Canadian or Maine forests. On cold days two light-weight union garments are warmer than one of heavy weight. Wool is never clammy and cold, it absorbs perspiration and when on the trail prevents the chilly feeling often experienced when halting for a rest in the forest.

Union garments may be obtained in a variety of weights, and a one-piece suit is the only garment necessary to wear under bloomers and middy when at camp.

Leave corsets at home, they have no place in the outdoor life, and you will be freer if you discard the dress skirt when at camp and on the trail. Have your muscles free, be able to take in long, deep breaths, to move readily all portions of your body, and not be hampered in any way by ill-fitting, uncomfortable clothing. There must be unrestricted freedom of arms and limbs for a girl to be able to use them easily in climbing mountains or hills, scrambling over fallen trees, sliding over rocks, jumping from stone to stone, or from root to half-sunken log on wet trails of the forest.

Stockings
Select your stockings with care. Let them be of wool, strong, soft, and absolutely satisfactory when the shoe is on. The aim of the entire camp dress is to have it so comfortable and well adapted to outdoor life that you will forget it; think no more of it than a bird does of its feathers. When woollen stockings are worn, wet feet are not apt to give one cold, for the feet do not become chilled even when it is necessary to stand in the reedy edge of a mountain lake or stream. If, however, you cannot wear wool, use cotton stockings. Remember that wool often shrinks in the wash. Allow for this when purchasing goods, though it is said, on reliable authority, that if laundered with care the garments will not shrink.

When washing woollen underwear use very soapy, cool water (not icy) with addition of a little borax, or ammonia, if you have either, and do not rub soap directly on wool; it mats the little fibres and this causes the wool to shrink. For the same reason avoid rubbing the garments if possible during the cleansing process. All that is usually necessary is to squeeze and souse them well, then rinse in water of the same temperature; do not wring the things; squeeze them and hang them up to dry. Changes of temperature in the water when washing wool will cause the wool to shrink. To alternate between cold and warm, hot and lukewarm water will surely cause the clothing to grow much smaller and stiffer; keep both wash and rinse water either cold or lukewarm; cold is safer.

Allow no one to persuade you to take old clothes to camp; they will soon need mending and prove a torment.

Shoes
Wear low-heeled, high-laced shoes of stout leather and easy fit. Make them water-proof by giving the leather a good coat of hot, melted mutton tallow, completely covering the shoes and working the tallow into all crevices. Be sure to do this, as it is worse than useless to depend upon rubber overshoes when trailing; sharp stones cut, and roots, twigs, and underbrush tear the rubber, with the result that the overshoes soon fill with water and your feet swim in little lakes. Test your shoes well before taking them to camp, be perfectly satisfied that they are comfortable and well-fitting, wear them steadily for one week or more. It is very unwise to risk new shoes on the trail, and it is of the utmost importance that the feet be kept in good condition. Be kind to your feet.

Camping Dress
The most serviceable and practical dress for camping is a three-piece suit, made of a fadeless, soft quality of gray or brown material.

DUFFEL-BAGS

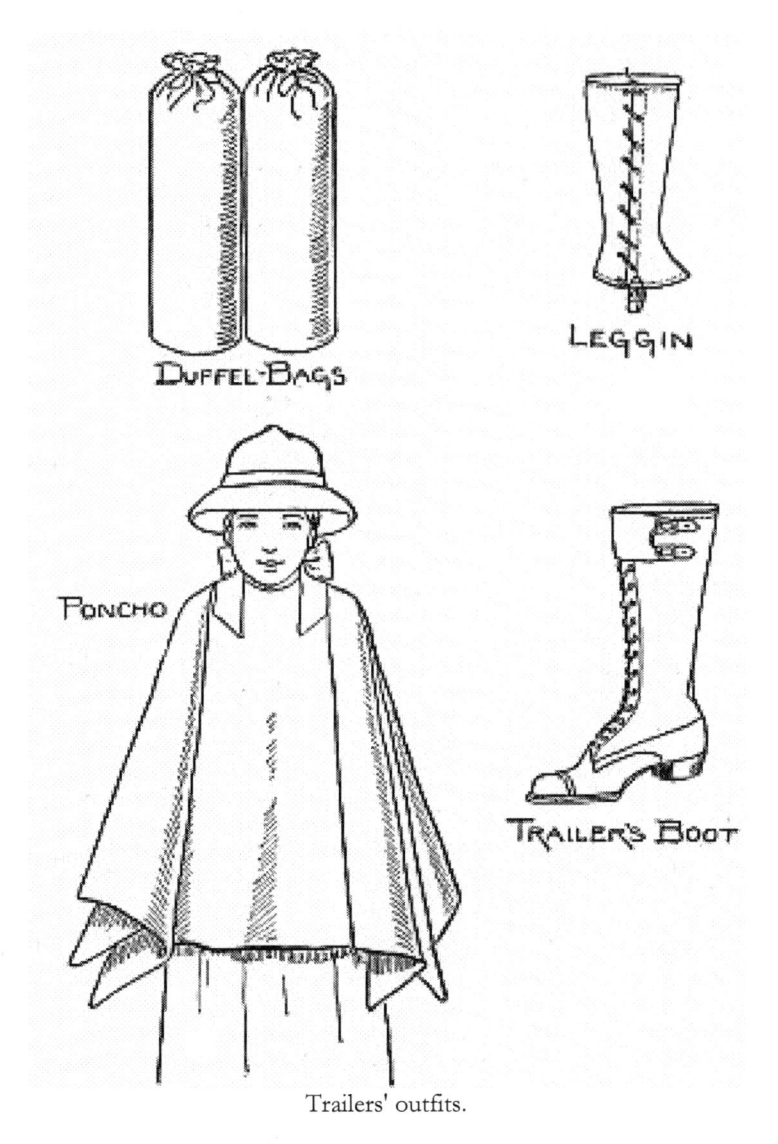

LEGGIN

PONCHO

TRAILER'S BOOT

Trailers' outfits.

The middy-blouse while loose can be well-fitting, with long sleeves roomy enough to allow of pushing up above the elbow when desired. Sew two small patch pockets high on the left breast—one for your watch, the other for your compass; protect the pockets with flaps which fasten down over the open top with dress snaps. On the right breast sew one good-sized pocket.

In addition to these you will need one large pocket on both right and left side of middy, below belt line, making in all three large and two small pockets. The belt is held in place by sliding it through loops sewed on the middy, one at the back and one on each side.

Make the skirt of this suit short enough for ease and of generous width, not to draw at front, but give perfect freedom of the limbs. Have a seam pocket in each side of the front breadth, and fasten the skirt down one side from belt to hem. It can then be quickly removed and used as a cape or a wind break when occasion requires. The bloomers, well-fitting and comfortable, gathered below the knee with best quality of elastic, that it may last, can have a deep pocket sewed across the front of each leg, several inches conveniently below waist-line.

Hat

A soft, light-weight felt hat with brim sufficiently wide to shade the eyes will prove the best head covering for the trail. Don't use hatpins; your hat will cling to the head if you substitute a strip of woollen cloth in place of the inside leather band. The clinging wool prevents the hat from being readily knocked off by overhanging branches or blown off on windy days.

Check List of Apparel

Go light when off for the woods, take with you only those things which seem to be absolutely necessary; remember that you will carry your own pack and be your own laundress, so hesitate about including too many washable garments. Make out your list, then consider the matter carefully and realize that every one of the articles, even the very smallest, has a way of growing heavier and heavier and adding to the ever-increasing weight of your pack the longer you walk, so be wise, read over your list and cut it down, decide that you *can* do without a number of things thought at first to be indispensable.

In addition to your camp dress described, the following list forms a basis to work upon, to be added to, taken from, or substitution made according to location, climate, and nature of the country where you will pitch camp:

One extra suit of wool underwear. Wash suit as soon as changed.

One extra pair of stockings. Every morning put on a fresh pair, washing the discarded ones the same day.

One high-necked, long-sleeved, soft, woven undershirt for cold days.

One extra thin middy-blouse for hot days.

Three pocket handkerchiefs, each laundered as soon as discarded.

One kimono, soft, warm wool, buttoned down front, not eider-down (it is too bulky), color brown or dark gray.

One bathing-suit without skirt, made in one-piece, loose, belted waist with bloomers; suit opened on shoulders with strong button and buttonhole fastenings.

One warm sweater with high turned-over collar and sleeves good and long. On the trail carry your sweater by tying the sleeves around your waist, allowing the sweater to hang down at the back.

One pair of gloves, strong, pliable, easy-fitting chamois, if you feel that you need them. The bare, free hands are better.

One pair of strong, snug, well-fitting leggins matching camp dress in color, with no buttons or buckles to tangle on underbrush. The fastening can be covered by smooth outer flap.

One pair of felt slippers or thick-soled moccasins for tent.

Four extra strips of elastic for renewing those in knees of bloomers.

One large, strong, soft silk or cotton neckerchief, for protecting neck from sun, rain, and cold, also good to fold diagonally and use for arm sling or tie over hat in a hard wind; silk is best.

Two head-nets if your stay is long, one if short, to be worn in case of swarms of pestiferous flies and mosquitoes. Especially needed for protection from the midge, black-fly, etc., found in northern forests and elsewhere during the spring and through to the middle or last of July. Your net can be of fine mesh bobbinet; if you have only white, dye it black; all other colors are apt to dazzle the eyes. The best material to use is black Brussels net. Cut a strip of net long enough to fit easily around your shoulders and allow of some fulness. Take the measurement smoothly around the shoulders with a piece of tape and add to this about three-eighths of the entire length you have just measured, which will give you the length required. The width should be sufficient to allow of the net reaching from base of hat crown across over brim and down over top of shoulders, about twenty-two inches or more in all. Cut the net according to size needed; then fold the strip at centre across the width, fold again, making four even folds. Once more fold and you will have divided the net into eight equal parts. Mark the net at each fold and open it out (Fig. 30). Cut armholes in the divisions marked 2 (Fig. 30) to fit over the shoulders, sew together the two ends, bind the shoulder armholes holding the net loosely that it may not pull and strain. Sew an elastic to back corner of each armhole, hem the top of net strip and run an elastic through hem to fit snugly on base of hat crown. Gather lower edges of net; then try the net on, adjusting lower and upper gathers so that the veil will blouse a little, remembering not to let the net touch your face; if it should, the little tormentors will bite through and torture you. Sew a piece of black tape across lower edge of the front and another across lower edge of the back, fitting the tape to lie smoothly over chest and back; then bring forward the hanging pieces of elastic, adjust them comfortably under the arms, and mark length of elastic to reach around under arm and fasten with dress snaps at front corner of armhole. Cut elastic and finish net (Fig. 30).

Ornaments—Never take rings, bracelets, necklaces, or jewelry of any kind to camp; leave all such things at home, and with them ribbons, beads, and ornaments of all descriptions.

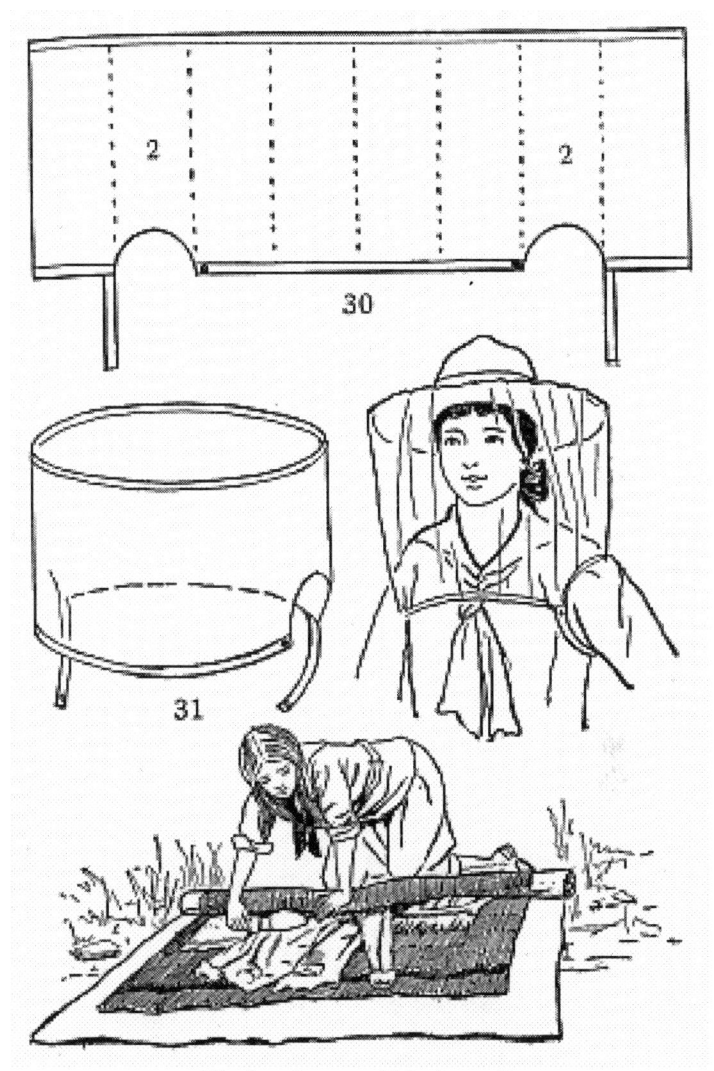

The head-net and blanket-roll.

Check List of Toilet Articles
One comb, not silver-backed.

One hand-mirror to hang or stand up.

One tooth-brush in case.

One tube of tooth-paste, or its equivalent.

One nail-brush.

One cake of unscented toilet-soap.

Two cakes of laundry-soap.

One package of borax or securely corked bottle of ammonia.

One tube of cold-cream.

One baking-powder can of pure, freshly "tried out" mutton tallow, made so by boiling in pure water until melted, then allowed to cool and harden. When taken from the water, again melted and, while hot, strained through a clean cloth into the can. Good to remove pitch and balsam-gum from the hands, to use as cold-cream to soften the hands, and excellent to water-proof the shoes.

One wash-cloth, washed, aired, and sunned every day. In rainy weather, washed and dried.

Two hand towels, each washed as soon as soiled.

One bath towel, washed as soon as used.

One manicure-scissors.

One package sandpaper nail-files.

Two papers of hair-pins.

One paper of common pins, also little flat pocket pincushion well filled around edge with pins.

Two papers of large-sized safety-pins.

Check List of Personal Camp Property
One note-book and pencil for taking notes on wild birds, animals, trees, etc.

One needle-case, compact with needles and strong white and black thread, wound on cardboard reels (spools are too bulky). Scissors, thimble, and large-eyed tape-needle for running elastic through hem in bloomers and head-net, when needed.

Two papers of very large sized safety-pins of horse-blanket kind

One roll of tape, most useful in many ways.

One whistle, the loudest and shrillest to be found, worn on cord around the neck, for calling help when lost or in case of need. A short, simple system of signalling calls should be adopted.

One compass, durable and absolutely true.

One watch, inexpensive but trustworthy. Do not take your gold watch.

One package of common post-cards, with lead pencil attached. The postals to take the place of letters.

One package writing-paper and stamped envelopes, if post-cards do not meet the needs.

One pocket-knife, a big, strong one, with substantial, sharp, strong blades, for outdoor work and to use at meals.

One loaded camera, in case which has secure leather loops through which your belt can be slipped to carry camera and hold it steady, leaving the hands free and precluding danger of smashing the instrument should a misstep on mossy stone or a trip over unseen vine or root suddenly throw you down and send the camera sailing on a distance ahead. Such an accident befell a girl camper who was too sure that her precious camera would be safest if carried in her hand. Wear the camera well back that you may not fall on it should you stumble, or the camera can be carried on strap slung from the right shoulder.

Three or more rolls of extra films, the quantity depending upon your length of stay at camp and the possibilities for interesting subjects.

One fishing-rod and fishing-tackle outfit. Choose the simple and useful rather than the fancy and expensive. Select your outfit according to the particular kind of fishing you will find near camp. There is a certain different style of rod and tackle for almost every variety of fish. If fishing is not to be a prominent feature of the camp, you might take line and hooks, and wait until you reach camp to cut your fishing-pole.

One tin cup, with open handle to slide over belt. The cup will serve you with cool sparkling water, with cocoa, coffee, or tea as the case may be, and it will also be your soup bowl. Keep the inside of the cup bright and shiny. While aluminum is much lighter than other metal, it is not advisable to take to camp either cup, teaspoon, or fork of aluminum because it is such a good conductor of heat that those articles would be very apt to burn your lips if used with hot foods.

One dinner knife, if you object to using your pocket-knife.

One dinner fork, not silver.

One teaspoon, not silver.

One plate, may be of aluminum or tin, can be kept bright by scouring with soap and earth.

Two warm wool double blankets, closely woven and of good size. The U.S. Army blankets are of the best. With safety-pins blankets can be turned into sleeping-bags and hammocks.

One poncho, light in weight to wear over shoulders, spread on ground rubber side down to protect from dampness, can be used in various ways.

One pillow-bag.

One mattress-bag.

One water-proof match-safe.

One belt hatchet in case, or belt sheath small axe, for chopping wood and felling small trees, but, be very careful when using either of these tools. Before going to camp find some one who can give you proper instructions in handling one or both, and practise carefully following directions. Be very *cautious* and go slow until you become an expert. Outdoor books and magazines should be consulted for information, and if you do not feel absolutely confident of your ability to use the hatchet or axe after practising, *do not take them with you*. For the sake of others as well as yourself, you have not the right to take chances of injuring either others or yourself through inability to use safely any tool. Do not attempt to use a regular-sized axe, it is very dangerous. One guide told me that after a tenderfoot chopped a cruel gash nearly through his foot when using the guide's axe, that axe was never again loaned, but kept in a safe place and not allowed to be touched by any one except the owner.

Check List for First Aid
One hot-water bag, good for all pains and aches, and a comfort when one is chilly.

One package pure ginger pulverized or ground, to make hot ginger tea in case of chill, pains in the bowels, or when you have met with an accidental ducking or are wet through to the skin by rain. Never mind if the tea does burn, ginger always stings when helping one. Be a good sport, take your medicine.

One box of charcoal tablets for dyspepsia or indigestion.

One package bicarbonate of soda (baking-soda); good for burns, sprinkle well with soda, see that the burn is completely covered, then cover lightly with cloth, and do not disturb it for a long time.

One bottle of ammonia well corked. Tie the cork down firmly in the bottle (Fig. 32); a flannel case or raffia covering will protect the glass from breakage. Good to smell in case of faintness, but care must be taken *not* to hold it *too near* the *nose*, as the ammonia might injure the delicate membranes, as would also smelling-salts. Safer to move the bottle or cloth wet with ammonia slowly back and forth near the nose. Good also for insect bites.

One roll of adhesive plaster. Cut into lengths for holding covered ointment or poultice in place, the strips criss-cross over the poultice, but are not attached, the ends only are pressed on the bare skin to which they firmly adhere.

Two rolls of 2-½ or 3 inch wide surgeon bandages (not gauze) for general use where bandages are needed.

One small package of absorbent cotton.

Two mustard plasters, purchased at drug store; good for stomachache.

One package of powdered licorice to use as a laxative. Dissolve a little licorice in water and drink it. To keep the bowels open means to ward off a host of evils. It is even more essential that the inside of the body be kept clean than it is to have the outside clean. To this end make a practise of drinking a great deal of pure water; drink it before breakfast, between meals (not at meals), and before retiring. If you do this, you will probably not need other laxative, especially if you eat fruit either fresh or stewed. Fruit should form part of every day's fare. *Keep your bowels open.*

One tube of Carron oil, to use for burns or scalds.

One small bottle of camphor, for headaches.

One small bag of salt—good dissolved in water, 1 teaspoonful to 1 pint of water, for bathing tired or inflamed eyes, often effects a cure. Good for bathing affected spots of ivy poison, good for sore-throat gargle, also for nosebleed; snuff, then plug nose. Good for brushing teeth. For all these dissolve salt in water in proportion as given above.

One white muslin 24-inch triangular bandage, for arm sling or chest, jaw, and head bandage. A man's large-sized white handkerchief can be used; never bind broken skin with colored cloth.

One bottle of fly dope, warranted to keep off pestiferous flies and mosquitoes. All these may be kept in one-half of a linen case of pockets, your toilet articles in the other half, and the case can be opened out and hung to the side of your tent or shelter.

Check List for General Camp
Two basins, of light metal, paper or collapsible rubber. The last is easy to pack and light to carry. One basin will serve for several girls. If you camp near a body of fresh water let that be your basin; it will always be ready filled. No need then to bring water to your shelter, for a delightful dip in the river or lake every morning before breakfast will obviate all necessity, and do away with the otherwise needful hand-basin.

One reliable map of location and surrounding country for constant reference.

One water-pail, light weight, for every two or three girls. Can be canvas, aluminum, paper, rubber, or your own selection in other materials.

Six toilet-paper packages or more.

One or more tents of water-proof material.

One or more sod cloths for tent flooring.

One or more inner tents of cheesecloth for protection from mosquitoes, etc. These can be made at home or purchased with the tents at the regular camp-outfitters'. There is on the market a spray, claimed to be absolutely effective against mosquitoes, etc., and to keep both tent and camp free from pests. One quart is said to last two weeks with daily use. Cost, fifty cents per quart.

One carborundum stone for sharpening all cutting tools.

One or more lanterns. Folding candle lanterns may be purchased, but the simple ten-cent kind with lamp-chimney for protection of candle are good. They can be had at country stores in Cresco, Pa. May possibly be found at camp-outfitters'. If a glass chimney is to be used, pack most carefully. Fill the inside of the chimney with stockings, handkerchiefs, etc.; then wrap the chimney all over with other soft clothing and tie securely. Have this outside wrap very thick.

One package of one-half length candles to use in lantern.

One *tin* box of one or two dozen safety-matches. *Tin* will not catch fire from the matches.

One strong tool-bag with separate labelled pockets for different tools; each pocket with flap to fasten securely with dress snaps. In this tool-bag put assorted nails, mostly big, strong ones, screws, awl, well-sealed bottle of strong glue, ball of stout twine, a few rawhide thongs, three or four yards of soft strong rope, a pair of scissors, two spools of wire, and several yards of cheesecloth.

One rope—long for mountain-climbing.

Check List of Kitchen Utensils

Two dish-pans, one for piping-hot sudsy water for washing dishes, the other for scalding-hot rinsing water. The last pan can also be used for mixing and bread-making. Select pans strong and of light weight—canvas, aluminum, or tin—and be sure they nest or fold.

Two water-pails, fitted one within the other, both light weight

One coffee-pot, size to fit in pails, must not be too high. Cocoa can be made in the coffee-pot.

One frying-pan, for corn-dodgers, flapjacks, fried mush, eggs, etc.

One folding camp-oven, for hot biscuits, bread puddings, and many other good things relished by hungry campers.

One wash-basin, to be kept strictly for washing hands, when cooking.

One large spoon, for stirring and general use.

One kitchen-knife, suitable for cutting bread, carving meat, turning pancakes, etc.

One kitchen-fork, strong and big, but not a toasting-fork.

One Dutch oven pot, a strong seamless pot with cover, to use for baking, boiling, and stewing.

Three dish-towels, washed after every meal.

One dish mop or cloth, washed and dried after each meal; dry in sun when possible.

Four large cakes of soap.

One thick holder, for lifting pots. Hang this up in a certain place where it may always be found when needed.

One pepper and one salt shaker, small and light in weight.

One net air-bag, for meat, fish, and anything that must be kept fresh (Fig. 33) and protected from the flies. Use strong net and two or more hoops for the air-bag. With pincers you can twist the two ends of strong wire together and make the hoops of size large enough to hold the net out away from a large piece of meat. Cut the net long enough to stand above and hang below the meat. Gather the top edge tightly together and sew it fast; then sew the hoop near the top of the bag. Other hoops on either side of centre of bag and a hoop near bottom of bag, or sew only one hoop at the top and one at the bottom. Have strong draw-strings in the bottom of the bag, and fasten a pendent hook at the top to hold the meat hanging free inside of the bag. With copper wire attach a good-sized ring on top of the bag, wire it through the handle of the pendent hook and weld them together. When in use, the bag should be suspended high from the ground by means of a rope pulley run through the top ring and over the limb of a near-by tree. Similar air-bags can be obtained, if desired, from camp-outfitters.

When selecting cooking utensils for the camp, you will find those with detachable handles pack better and for that reason are desirable.

Do not forget that every check-list given may be reduced; don't think you must include all the items. For these lists give outfits for permanent as well as temporary camps. If you can manage with *one towel* by washing it every day, or evening, allowing it to dry during the night, one towel will be sufficient; leave the others at home. Drop from the various lists every article you can possibly dispense with and still be comfortable in camp.

If you wear the camp suit travelling from home to camp, its weight and bulk will be omitted from your camp pack, and be so much to your gain, and you will maintain a good appearance notwithstanding, for if well made and of proper fit the dress will be a suitable travelling costume.

Camp Packs

When you intend carrying your belongings and striking the trail either part or all the way to camp, the easiest method for portage is to stow the things in a regular pack and fasten the pack on your back by means of strong, long straps attached to the pack, and passed over your shoulders and under your arms.

A square of water-proof canvas makes a simple and good camp pack. Get a nine-by-nine-feet (more or less) square of cloth, and it will be found useful as shelter, fly, ground-cloth, windbreak, and in other ways after reaching camp.

What to Put in Your Pack

Open out your pack-cloth flat on the floor, and place your folded mattress-bag in the centre.

Fill the pillow-bag with your first-aid case and case of toilet articles, and if there is space for other things pack them in. Lay the pillow-bag on top of the mattress-bag, place clothing by the side and on top of the pillow-bag, being careful to keep the contents of your pack rectangular in shape and of size to fit well over your back.

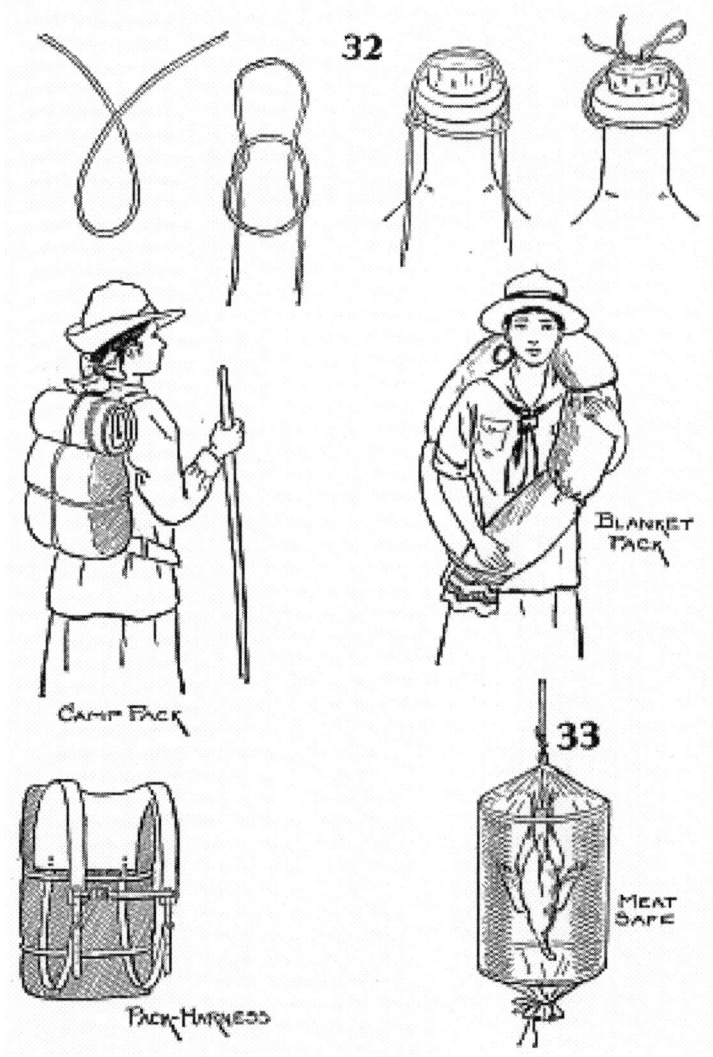

Some things to carry and how to carry them.

If not adding too much to the weight, include many things from your personal-belonging list; of these articles you can carry some in the pockets of your camp suit. Everything being in the pack, fold over the sides and ends, making a neat, compact bundle; tie it securely with a piece of soft rope and across its top place the blankets with poncho inside, which you have previously made into a roll to fit. Bind pack and blankets together, attach the pack shoulder-strap and swing the pack on your back.

Pack straps or harness can be obtained at any camp-outfitter's.

A different style of pack may be a bag with square corners, all seams strongly stitched, then bound with strong tape. Cut two pieces of the water-proof cloth, one about sixteen inches wide, and the other eighteen inches; this last is for the front and allows more space. Let each piece be twenty-one inches long or longer, unite them with a strip of the cloth six inches wide and sufficiently long to allow of flaps extending free at the top to fold over from both sides across the opening; you will then have a box-like bag. Make one large flap of width to fit the top of the back, and length to cross over on front, covering the smaller flaps and fastening down on the outside of the front of the pack. All three flaps may have pockets to hold small articles.

The shoulder-straps may be either of strong government webbing which comes for the purpose, tube lamp-wick, or leather.

With this pack the blanket and poncho could be made into a thin roll and fitted around the edges of the pack, or made into a short roll and attached to top of pack.

When feasible it is a good plan to pack your smaller belongings in wall-pockets with divisions protected by flaps securely fastened over the open ends, the wall-pockets rolled, tied, and carried in the camp pack. These pockets are useful at camp; they help to keep your things where you can find them. Next best is to use small separate labelled bags for different variety of duffel, and pack them in one or two duffel tube-shaped bags, which may be bound together, constituting one pack.

From eighteen to twenty-four pounds is average weight for a girl to carry; it all depends upon strength and endurance; some girls can carry even heavier packs, while others must have lighter ones. Beware about loading yourself down too heavily. Packs grow heavier and heavier, never lighter on the trail.

Blanket-Roll Pack

Side-trips from camp for only one night's bivouac will not need a back pack; the few articles required can be carried in your blanket-roll. Spread the poncho out flat, rubber side down, then your blankets on top, and group the things you intend to take into two separate oblong groups, one on each side of the central space at one end of the blankets; push the articles in each division closely together, leaving the space between the divisions empty. Kneel in front of your blankets and begin to roll all together tightly, taking care not to allow any of the duffel to fall out. When the roll is complete, tie the centre with strong, soft string, and also each end, and make a hoop of the roll by tying together the hanging strings on the two ends. Wear the blanket-roll over left shoulder, diagonally across back and chest to rest over right hip. If you have forgotten a few items, tie the things to the bottom of the blanket-roll and let them hang like tassels.

Duffel-Bag

Articles for general use while at camp can be packed together in one or more duffel-bags; if but one bag is needed, provisions might go in the same receptacle when space and weight permit. It is much better, however, to have a separate bag for provisions.

Packing Provisions

You can make or buy separate tube bags of different heights, but all of the same diameter, and pack flour in one, corn-meal in another, and so on, having each bag labelled and all, when filled, fitted in one duffel-bag; you will find these bags a great comfort. They should be of water-proof canvas with draw-string at the top. You can purchase friction-top cans for butter, etc., of varying depth to accommodate different quantities which will fit well in the large provision bag.

A duffel-bag is usually made cylindrical in form with a disk of the cloth sewed in tight at one end, and the other end closed with draw-strings. It is well to have another cloth disk attached to one spot at the top of the bag, to cover the contents before the draw-strings are fastened.

A great variety of desirable camp packs, including duffel-bags, pack-straps, harness, and tump-lines, may be purchased at the camp-outfitter's; investigate before deciding upon home-made camp packs. Pack-baskets can also be obtained, but all the good-sized pack-baskets I have seen, while attractive in appearance, are too rigid, bulky, sharp-edged, and heavy to be of use to girl campers.

Having decided that the wilderness is the place to locate, unless you can manage to camp with very little in the way of extra packs, you will be obliged to employ a guide to assist in the carry, possibly two guides, as wilderness trails do not permit of a vehicle, or even a mule or horse, being used to help in the portage.

Should your camp be on a more accessible site, the easy portage can be taken advantage of and the problem readily solved; but the charm of the real forest camp with all its possibilities for genuine life in the wilderness more, far more, than compensates for the extra difficulties in reaching camp. Really, though, the very difficulties are but part of the sport; they give zest and add to the fun of the trail.

CHAPTER V
OUTDOOR HANDICRAFT

Camp Furnishings—Dressing-Table, Seats, Dining-Table, Cupboard, Broom, Chair, Racks, Birch-Bark Dishes, etc.

Camp is the place where girls enjoy most proving their powers of resourcefulness.

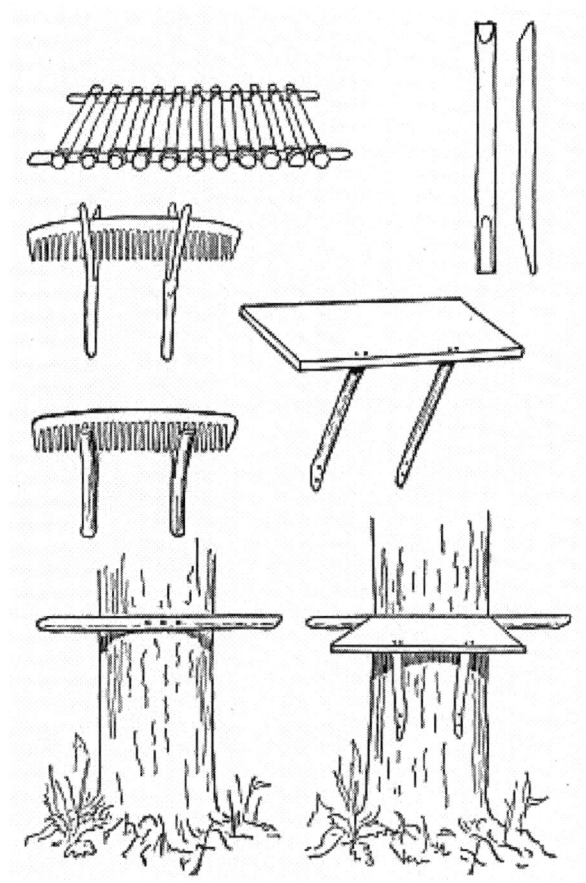

Handicraft in the woods.

Details of the outdoor dressing-table. Comb-racks of forked sticks and of split sticks.

It is fun to supply a want with the mere natural raw materials found in the open, and when you succeed in making a useful article of outdoor things, the entire camp takes a pride in your work and the simple but practical and usable production gives a hundred per cent more pleasure than could a store article manufactured for the same purpose.

Be comfortable at camp. While it is good to live simply in the open, it is also good to be comfortable in the open, and with experience you will be surprised to find what a delightful life can be lived at camp with but few belongings and the simplest of camp furnishings. These last can, in a great measure, be made of tree branches and the various stuffs found in the woods.

Dressing-Table

A near-by tree will furnish the substantial foundation for your dressing-table and wash-stand combined. If you can find a side-piece of a wooden box, use it for the shelf and fasten this shelf on the trunk of a tree about two and one-half feet or more above the ground. Cut two rustic braces and nail the front of the shelf on the top ends of these supports; then nail a strip of wood across the tree as a cleat on which to rest the back of the shelf; fit the shelf on the cleat and nail the lower ends of the braces to the tree; strengthen the work still more by driving a strong, long nail on each side of the top centre of the back of shelf, diagonally down through the shelf, cleat, and into the tree.

It is not essential that the straight shelf edge fit perfectly to the rounded tree, but if you desire to have it so, mark a semicircle on the wood of size to fit the tree and whittle it out.

Should there be no piece of box for your shelf, make the shelf of strong, slender sticks lashed securely close together on two side sticks. For cleats and braces use similar sticks described for board shelf.

When the shelf is made in this way, cover the top with birch bark or other bark to give a flat surface.

Hang your mirror on a nail in the tree at convenient distance above the shelf, and your tooth-brush on another nail. The towel may hang over the extending end of the cleat, and you can make a small bark dish for the soap. Your comb can rest on two forked-stick supports tacked on the tree, or two split-end sticks.

Camp-Seats

Stones, logs, stumps, raised outstanding roots of trees, and boxes, when obtainable, must be your outdoor chairs, stools, and seats until others can be made.

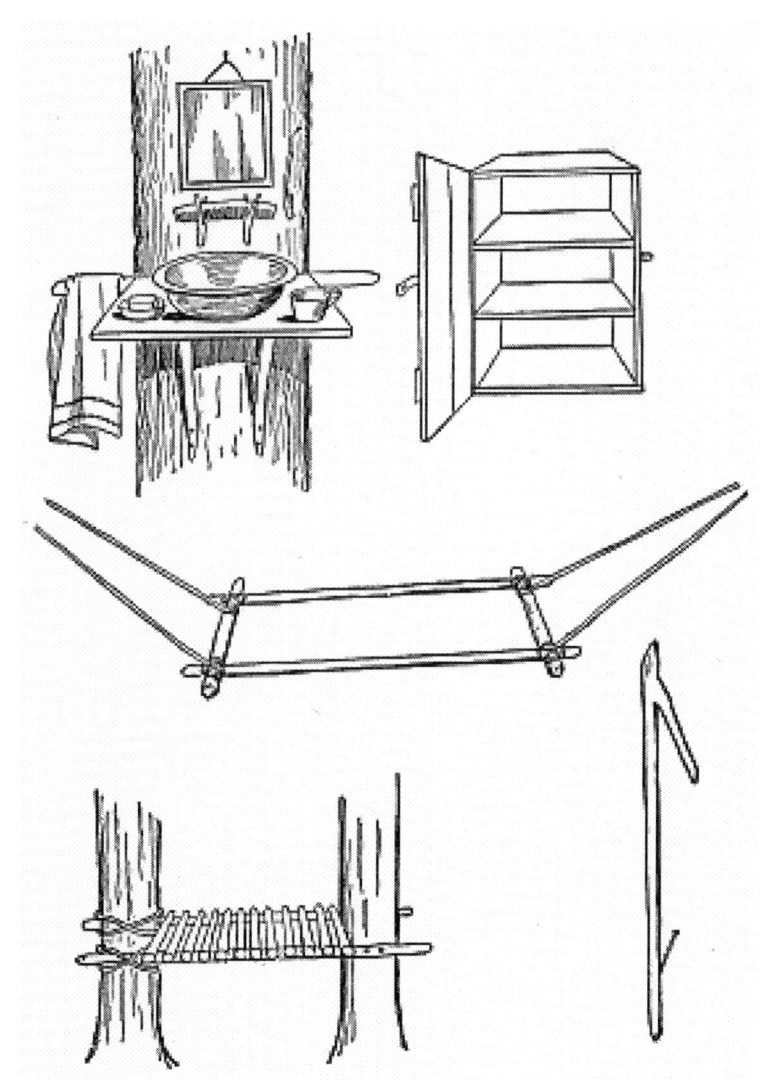

Outdoor dressing-table, camp-cupboard, hammock-frame, seat, and pot-hook.

Two trees standing near together may be used to advantage as uprights for a camp seat. Cut a small horizontal kerf or notch at the same height on opposite sides of both trees, get two strong poles (green wood), fit them in the wedges and nail them to the trees; then lash them firmly in place. Be absolutely certain that these poles are of strong wood, firmly attached to the trees and not liable to slide or break. Make the seat by lashing sticks across from pole to pole, placing them close together. Two more long poles, fastened to the trees at a proper distance above the seat, would give a straight back, if a back is desired, but it is not essential; with a folded blanket spread over it, the seat alone is a luxury.

Camp-Table
A table can be built in much the same way as the seat and will answer the purpose well if one of boards is not to be had. For the table make your crosspieces about twenty-two inches long, nail them ladder-like but close together on two poles, and make this table top flat on the surface by covering it with birch bark tacked on smoothly. Having previously

fastened two other poles across from tree to tree, as you did when making the seat, you can lift the table top and lay it on the two foundation poles; then bind it in place and the table will be finished. Another way of using the table top is to drive four strong, stout, forked sticks into the ground for the four table legs and place the table top across, resting the long side poles in the crotches of the stakes, where they may be lashed in place.

Benches for the table can be made in like manner, only have the forked-stick legs shorter, raising the seat about eighteen inches above the ground.

Camp-chair, biscuit-stick, and blanket camp-bed.

Camp-Cupboard
A cupboard made of a wooden box by inserting shelves, held up by means of cleats, will be found very convenient when nailed to a tree near the cook-fire. Hang a door on the cupboard which will close tight and fasten securely. Have this in mind when making out your check list, and add hinges, with screws to fit, to your camp tools.

Camp-Broom
With a slender pole as a handle, hickory shoots, or twisted fibre of inner bark of slippery-elm, for twine, and a thick bunch of the top branchlets of balsam, spruce, hemlock, or pine for the brush part, you can make a broom by binding the heavy ends of the branches tight to an encircling groove cut on the handle some three inches from the end. Cut the bottom of the brush even and straight.

Camp-Chair
If you have a good-size length of canvas or other strong cloth, make a camp-chair. For the back use two strong, forked stakes standing upright, and use two long poles with branching stubs at equal distance from the bottom, for the sides and front legs of the chair; in the crotches of these stubs the bottom stick on which the canvas strip is fastened will rest.
Each side pole must be fitted into one of the forked high-back stakes, and then the top stick on the canvas strip must be placed in the same crotches, but in front of and resting against the side poles, thus locking the side poles firmly in place.
To fasten the canvas on the two sticks, cut one stick to fit across the chair-back and the other to fit across the lower front stubs. Fold one end of the canvas strip over one stick and nail the canvas on it, so arranging the cloth that the row of nails will come on the under side of the stick. Turn in the edge first that the nails may go through the double thickness of cloth. Adjust this canvas-cov ered stick to the top of the chair, allowing the cloth to form a loose hanging seat; measure the length needed for back and seat, cut it off and nail the loose end of the canvas strip to the other stick; then fit one stick in the top of the upright back stakes and the other stick in the bottom stubs.

Camp Clothes-Press
If you are in a tent tie a hanging pole from the tent ridge-pole, and use it as a clothes-press.

Blanket Bed
Two short logs will be required for your blanket bed, the thicker the better, one for the head and one for the foot, also two long, strong, green-wood poles, one for each side of the bed; your blanket will be the mattress.
Fold the blanket, making the seam, formed by bringing the two ends together, run on the under-side along the centre of the doubled blanket, not on the edge. Lap and fasten the blanket ends together with large horse-blanket safety-pins, and with the same kind of pins make a case on each side of the blanket fold; then run one of the poles through each case. Chop a notch near each end of the two short logs; in these notches place the ends of the poles and nail them securely. Have the short logs thick enough to raise the bed up a few inches from the ground, and make the notches sufficiently far apart to stretch the mattress out smooth, not have it sag. A strip of canvas or khaki may be used in place of the blanket if preferred.

Camp Hammock
By lashing short crosspieces to the head and foot of the side poles the blanket mattress can be a hammock and swing between two trees, having been attached to them with rope or straps of slippery-elm, beech, or black birch.

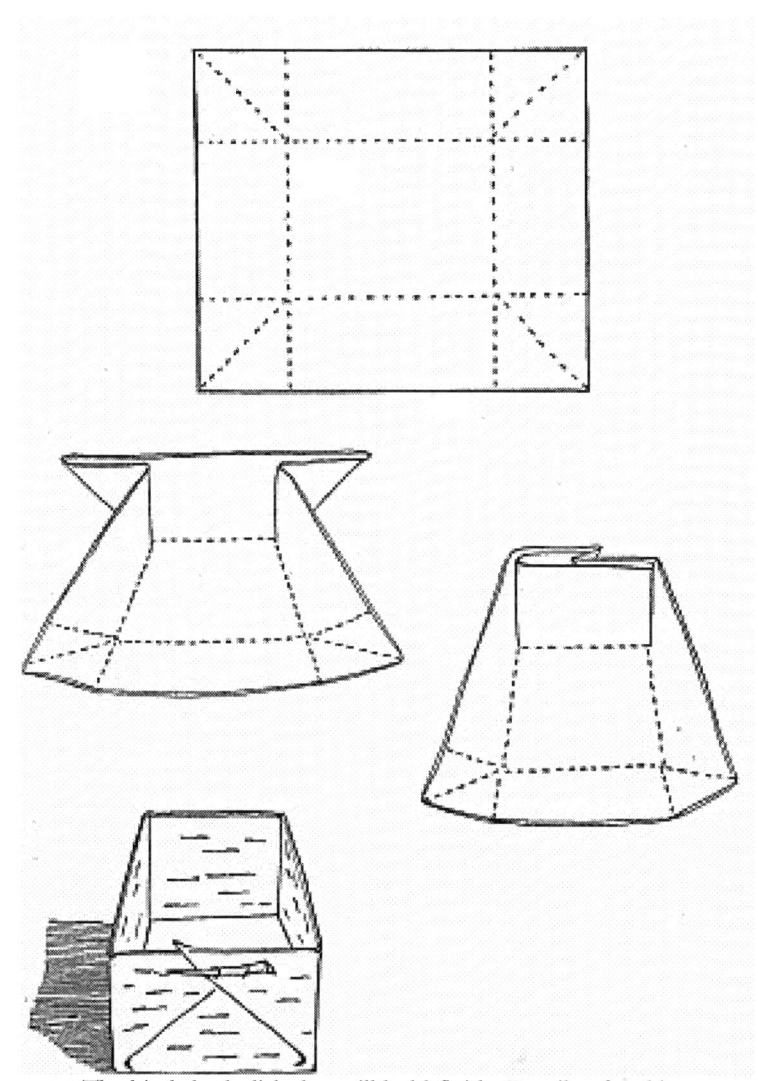

The birch-bark dish that will hold fluids. Details of making.

Birch-Bark Dishes

It will be easy for girls to make their birch-bark dinner plates, vegetable dishes, baskets, dippers, etc. Soften the thick bark by soaking it in water; when it is pliable cut one plate the size you wish, lay it on a flat stone or other hard substance and scrape off the outside bark around the edges, allowing the outer bark to remain on the bottom of the plate to give greater strength; use this plate as a guide in cutting each of the others.

With your fingers shape the edges of the plates in an upward turn while the bark is wet, using the smoothest side for the inside of the plate.

A large bark cornucopia with bark strap-handle can be made and carried on the arm in place of a basket when off berrying.

Variations of circular, oblong, and rectangular bark dishes may be worked out from strips and rectangular pieces of birch bark, and all dishes can be turned into baskets by adding handles. When necessary to sew the edges of bark together, always have the bark wet and soft; then lap the edges and use a very coarse darning-needle with twine of inner-bark fibre or rootlets; have ready hot melted grease mixed with spruce gum to coat over the stitching and edges of the article, or you can use white-birch resin for the same purpose.

The bark utensils will wear longer if a slender rootlet or branchlet of pliable wood is sewed, with the "over-and-over" stitch, to the edge of the article.

For round and oblong dishes or baskets, sew together the two ends of your strip of wet bark; then sew the round or oblong bottom on the lower edge of the bark circle. In this case it is not easy to lap the edges, simply bring them together and finish the seam with the addition of the slender rootlet binding. Rectangular dishes are made by folding the wet bark according to the diagrams and fastening the folds near the top of both ends of the receptacle. These will hold liquids.

Cooking Utensils

A forked stick with points sharpened makes a fine toasting-fork or broiling-stick for bacon or other small pieces of meat. The meat is stuck on the two prongs and held over the fire.

A split-end stick may be used for the same purpose by wedging the bacon in between the two sides of the split.

Your rolling-pin can be a peeled, straight, smooth, round stick, and a similar stick, not necessarily straight but longer, may do duty as a biscuit baker when a strip of dough is wound spirally around it and held over the fire.

A hot flat stone can also be used for baking biscuits, and a large flat-topped rock makes a substitute for table and bread-board combined.

If you have canned goods, save every tin can when empty, melt off the top, and with nail and hammer puncture a hole on two opposite sides near the top, and fasten in a rootlet handle. These cans make very serviceable and useful cooking-pails.

Whittle out a long-handled cake-turner from a piece of thin split wood, and also whittle out a large flat fork.

Make a number of pot-hooks of different lengths, they are constantly needed at camp; select strong green sticks with a crotch on one end and drive a nail slantingly into the wood near the bottom of the stick on which to hang kettles, pots, etc. Be sure to have the nail turn up and the short side of the crotch turn down as in diagram.

Campers employ various methods of making candlesticks. One method is to lash a candle to the side of the top of a stake driven into the ground, or the stake can have a split across the centre of the top, and the candle held upright by a strip of bark wedged in the split with a loop on one side holding the candle and the two ends of the bark extending out beyond the other side of the stake. Again the candle is stuck into a little mound of clay, mud, or wet sand. If you have an old glass bottle, crack off the bottom by pouring a little water in the bottle and placing it for a short while on the fire embers; then plant your candle in the ground and slide the neck of the bottle over the candle. Steady it by planting the neck of the bottle a little way in the ground and the glass bottle will act as a windbreak for your candle.

Never leave a candle burning even for a moment unless some one is present; it is a dangerous experiment. Fire cannot be trifled with. *Put out* your candle before leaving it.

A good idea before going away from camp when vacation is over is to photograph all the different pieces of your outdoor handicraft, and when the prints are made label each one with the month, date, and year and state material used, time required in the making, and comments on the work by other camp members.

Be sure to take photographs of different views of the camp as a whole, also of each separate shelter, both the outside and the inside, and have pictures of all camp belongings.

The authors will be greatly interested in seeing these.

A bear would rather be your friend than your enemy.

CHAPTER VI
MAKING FRIENDS WITH THE OUTDOOR FOLK
In the Woods, the Fields, on the Shore. Stalking Animals and Birds

There is but one way to make friends with the folk of the wild, and that is by gentleness, kindness, and quietness. Also one must learn to be fearless. It is said that while animals may not understand our language they do understand, or feel, our attitude toward them; and if it is that of fear or dislike we stand little chance of really knowing them, to say nothing of establishing any kind of friendly relations with them. By quiet watchfulness, keenness of sight and hearing, you may obtain a certain amount of knowledge of their ways, but when you add real sympathy and kindly feeling you gain their confidence and friendship. Make them understand that you will not interfere with or harm them, and they will go about their own affairs unafraid in your presence. Then you may silently watch their manner of living, their often amusing habits, and their frank portrayal of character. As a guest in the wild, conducting yourself as a courteous guest should, you will be well treated by your wild hosts, some of whom, in time, may even permit you to feed and stroke them. They do not dislike but fear you; they would rather be your friends than your enemies. The baby animal which has not yet learned to fear a human being will sometimes, when in danger, run to you for protection. This must win your heart if nothing else can.

Making friends with a ruffed grouse.

Stalking

You may stalk an animal by remaining quiet as well as by following its trail. To even see some of the inhabitants of woods, fields, and shore you must be willing to exercise great patience and conform to their method of hiding by remaining absolutely still. It is the thing that moves that they fear. Some of the animals appear not even to see a person who remains motionless. At any rate, they ignore him as they do a stump or stone.

For this quiet stalking, find as comfortable a seat as you can where you have reason to think some kind of animal or animals will pass and resign yourself to immovable waiting. If the rock beneath you grows unreasonably hard or the tree roots develop sharp edges, or the ground sends up unnoticed stones of torment; if your foot "goes to sleep" or your nose itches, bear the annoyances bravely and your reward will be sure and ample. If the wait is unduly long and movement of some kind becomes imperative, let such movement be made so slowly as to be almost imperceptible. Remember that unseen, suspicious eyes will be attracted by any sudden action and the faintest sound will be heard, for these spell danger to the wilderness folk and if frightened away they are not apt to return.

Keep your ears open to detect the first sound of approaching life. There is a thrill in this experience, and another when the animal you have heard comes boldly out before you. Then it is you will find that, in some mysterious way, all bodily discomfort has vanished. Your whole being is absorbed in the movements of the creature who is unconscious of your presence, and there is no room for other sensations. More animals may appear and perhaps a little drama may be enacted as if for your benefit.

Found on the trail.

Chipmunk and white-footed mouse, panther, kangaroo rat, raccoon, and weasel. It may be a tragedy, it may be a comedy, or it may be only a bit of every-day family life; but you do not know the plot nor how many actors will take part, and your very uncertainty adds zest to the situation.

Animals Found on the Trail

The animals most frequently seen in the woods where there is no longer any large game are the chipmunk, the red, the gray, and the black squirrel, the rabbit and hare, the fox, weasel, pine-marten, woodchuck, raccoon, opossum, and skunk, also the pack-rat (of the west), the white-footed and field mouse. In deeper and wilder forests there are deer and porcupine, though deer are found quite near habitations at times. In more remote places there are the moose and caribou; the bear, mountain-lion, lynx or wildcat, and the timber-wolf. The wolf is, however, equally at home in the open and at this day is most plentiful on the wide plains of the west. Unless your trail leads through the remote wilderness, you will hardly come across the more savage animals, and when you do invade their territory it will give you greater courage to call to mind the fact that they, as well as the smaller wild things, are afraid of man. Our most experienced hunters and our best writers on the subject of animal life agree that a wild animal's first emotion upon seeing a human being is undoubtedly *fear*. When you come upon one suddenly you may feel sure that he is as much frightened as you are and will probably turn aside to avoid you unless he thinks you are going to attack him. All wild creatures are afraid of fire, therefore the camp-fire is a barrier they will not pass, and a blazing firebrand will drive any of them away.

Timber wolves.

Birds

Among the feathered tribes of the woods you will find the owl, the woodcock, and the grouse. Of the smaller birds, the nuthatch, the wood and hermit thrush, whippoorwill, woodpeckers, wood-pewee, and others. Most of the birds prefer the edge of the woods, where they can dip into the sunshine and take long flights through the free air of the open; but the hermit-thrush, shyest and sweetest of singers, makes his home deep in the silent, shadowy forest. In these depths, and oftenest near a bog or marsh, you may also hear the call of the partridge, or more properly, the ruffed grouse. As given by the writer William J. Long, the call is like this:
"Prut, prut, pr-r-r-rt! Whit-kwit? Pr-r-r-rt, pr-r-r-rt! Ooo-it, ooo-it? Pr-r-reeee!"
Or perhaps you will be startled by the rolling drum-call. This begins slowly, increases rapidly, and ends something like this: "Dum! dum! dum! dum-dum-dum-dumdumdum!" The drum-call is made by the male bird who, beating the air with his wings, produces the sound. It is said to be a mating-call, but is heard at other times as well, long after the mating-season is over.

Baby moose.

Stalking the Ruffed Grouse
If you want to see the birds, stalk them when you hear their call. Wait until you locate the direction of the sound, then walk silently and follow it. As soon as the birds are sighted slip from one tree to another, stopping instantly when you think they may see you, until you can conceal yourself behind a bush, tree, or stump near enough for you to peer around and have a good view of your game. It may sometimes be necessary to drop to your knees in order to keep out of sight. If you have heard the drum it is the cock that you have stalked and, if early in the season, you will soon see his demure little mate steal through the underbrush to meet her lordly master as he stands proudly on an old log awaiting her. The "whit-kwit" call may lead you to the hen grouse with her brood of little chicks which are so much the color of the brown leaves you will not see them until they move. If the call comes later in the year you may come upon a flock of well-grown young birds who have left their mother and are now following a leader.

The ruffed grouse is a beautiful bird. He is yellowish-brown or rusty, splashed with black or dark brown, and white, with under-parts of a light buff. His beak is short and on his small, dainty head he carries his crest proudly. His shoulders bear epaulets of dark feathers, called the ruff, and his fan-like tail is banded and cross-barred. The nest of the grouse is on the ground, usually against a fallen log, at the foot of a tree, or in a hollow made by the roots; or it may be hidden amid underbrush. It is easily overlooked, being made of dry leaves with, perhaps, some feathers. In the season it contains from eight to fourteen eggs.

Woodcock
The woodcock, another forest bird, seldom shows himself in broad daylight except when hunted; then he will rise a few feet, fly a short distance, drop and run, hiding again as quickly as he can. You will know the woodcock from the ruffed grouse by his *long bill*, his short legs, and his very short tail. He frequents the banks of wooded streams or the bogs of the forests and, like the grouse, nests on the ground; but the woodcock's nest seldom contains more than four eggs.

Stalking wild birds.

Beaver

Along the shores of sluggish streams, of lonely lakes and ponds, you may see the beaver, the muskrat, very rarely the otter, and sometimes an ugly little, long-bodied animal belonging to the marten family called the fisher. These are all interesting, each in its own way, and well worth hours of quiet observation. The beaver, otter, and fisher choose wild, secluded places for their homes, but the muskrat may be found also in the marshes of farm lands. On the edges of our Long Island meadows the boys trap muskrats for their skins.

You will find the beaver house in the water close to the shore and overlapping it. Though strongly and carefully built, it looks very much like a jumble of small driftwood, with bleached sticks well packed together, and the ends standing out at all angles. The sticks are stripped of their bark and the house gleams whitely against the dark water. The houses vary in size, some being built as high as five feet. The beaver is rarely seen early in the day, most of his work is done at night, so the best time to watch for him is just before dusk or perhaps an hour before sundown. It is not well to wait to see the beaver if your trail back to camp is a long one, leading through dense forests. You would far better postpone making its acquaintance than to risk going over the, perhaps, treacherous paths after dark. Night comes early in the woods and darkness shuts down closely while it is still light in the open. If your camp is near the beaver house or beaver dam, or if your trip can be made by water, then, with no anxiety about your return, you can sit down and calmly await the coming of this most skilful of all building animals, and may see him add material to his house, or go on with his work of cutting down a tree, as a reward for your patience.

Fish-Hawk, Osprey
On the shore you will also find the fish-hawk, or osprey; a well-mannered bird he is said to be, who fishes diligently and attends strictly to his own business. The fish-hawk's nest will generally be at the top of a dead tree where no one may disturb or look into it, though, as the accompanying photograph shows, it is sometimes found on rocks near the ground. The young hawks have a way of their own of defending themselves from any climbing creature, and to investigators of the nest the results are disastrously disagreeable as well as laughable. As the intruder climbs near, the baby birds put their heads over the sides of the nest and empty their stomachs upon him. This is vouched for by a well-known writer who claims to have gone through the experience.

The female osprey is larger and stronger than the male. On slowly moving wings she sails over the water, dropping suddenly to clutch in her strong talons the fish her keen eyes have detected near the surface of the water. Fish are fish to the osprey and salt waters or fresh are the same to her. I have watched the bird plunge into the waves of the ocean, on the coast of Maine, to bring out a cunner almost too large for her to carry, and I have seen her drop into the placid waters of an Adirondack lake for lake-trout in the same manner.

Blue Heron
The great blue heron is one of the shore folk and his metallic blue-gray body gleams in the sunlight, as you sight him from your canoe, standing tall and slim, a lonely figure on the bank. He flies slowly and majestically, with his long legs streaming out behind. When out in a small boat on Puget Sound a large heron escorted us some distance. As we rowed near the shore he would fly ahead and then wait for us, standing solemnly on a stone in the water or a partially submerged log, to fly again as we approached.

The fish-hawk will sometimes build near the ground.

This escort business seems to be a habit of the heron family, for the same thing occurred on the Tomoca River, Fla., the home of the alligator, when a small, brilliantly blue heron flew ahead of our boat for several miles, always stopping to wait for us, and then going on again.

The heron is a fisher and when you see him standing close to the water, on one foot perhaps, he is awaiting his game. It matters not how long he must remain immovable, there he will stand until the fish comes within striking distance, when the long, curved neck will shoot out like a snake and the strong beak grasp its unwary prey.

Loon, Great Northern Diver

Another interesting bird, which you may both hear and see on secluded lakes, is the loon or great northern diver. I first heard the wild cry of the loon, a lonesome and eerie sound, on Pine River Pond, a small lake in the foot-hills of the White Mountains. There I saw the great bird dive and disappear beneath the water to remain an alarmingly long time, and then come up several hundred yards away, and rising, fly slowly to the shore. It is always a matter for guessing when the loon dives, for you can never tell where she will come up. This great diver is a large black-and-white bird, about the size of a goose. The breast is white, head black, and a white ring encircles its black neck. Its beak is long, its legs very short and placed far back on the body. It is essentially a water-bird, and on shore is both slow and awkward. I do not think it possible to become very intimate with the loon, for it is one of the wildest of our birds, and so suspicious it will allow no close approach, but quiet watching will reveal many of its interesting characteristics. Some one once found the nest of a loon and brought me a little, downy, young one that I might try to tame it; but it lived only a day or two in spite of all the devotion expended upon it, and its wild, frightened cry was too pathetic to allow of another experiment of the kind.

Animals and Birds of the Open

You will find that the wild life of the open differs in some respects from that of the woods, though there will be the woodchuck, the rabbit, the fox, and the hare in the fields and farm lands as well as in the woods. The weasel, too, makes unwelcome visits to the farm, but besides these there are other animals that are seldom or never found in the woods.

Field-Mouse

There is the little field-mouse, a short-eared and short-tailed little creature with a thick neck and of a red-brown color. It feeds on grain and seeds, and when hard pressed for food will also eat the bark of trees.

Kangaroo-Rat, Jumping Mouse

In the underbrush near a meadow and at the edges of thickets you may possibly see, though they are not common, a diminutive animal, beautiful in form and color and of most interesting habits. In the Southwest it is called the kangaroo-rat, but North and East it is known as the jumping mouse. The name kangaroo-rat is given because of its short fore legs, strong hind legs, and the kangaroo-like leaps it makes. In temper it is very unlike the ordinary rat; it does not bite and can be safely handled, but will not live if kept in captivity.

Pocket-Gopher

The pocket-gopher lives and burrows in the fields. It is a mole-like animal but much larger than the common mole. Its legs are short and its front feet strong, with long nails for digging. The fur is soft and silky and dark brown in color. Where the gopher is there may be found the weasel, his greatest enemy. It should be an even fight between them, for they are equally matched in ill-temper and savageness, and are near of a size though the gopher is the heavier.

Antelope

On the great plains of the west you may still see the beautiful and gentle antelope, though that animal is fast disappearing, while the thieving coyote thrives and multiplies in the same region.

Coyote, Prairie-Wolf

The coyote, or prairie-wolf, is about the size of a large dog and resembles one. Its color is gray, made by a mixture of black and white hairs. It is a cowardly animal and not dangerous, but its contemptible character could not prevent a wave of compassion that came over me when I saw one poor creature caged in a wooden box and holding up the bloody stump where its fore foot had been torn off by the cruel and barbarous steel trap.

Spermophile

In the Middle West, especially in Indiana, the little spermophile, sometimes called the ground-squirrel, is common and not afraid to venture into the outskirts of a village. One variety wears spotted brown and yellow stripes down its back, another is gray, but all are about the size of a gray squirrel. On the western prairies are the comical little prairie-dogs. You can see them sitting up on their haunches watching the train as it carries you over the great plains.

Antelopes of the western plains.

Bobolink
The birds of the open are varied and many. Most of the forest birds are seen occasionally in the fields, but some birds make their homes in the open. You will find the bobolink's nest in a hay-field or down among the red clover. The bobolink of the north is a sweet singer and is pretty in his black and white feathers with a touch of yellow at the back of his head. There are creamy-yellow feathers down his back, too, but they are not noticeable. When he goes south the male loses his pretty coat and, clad like his mate in yellowish-brown, is known as the rice-bird because he feeds on the rice crops. Here he is killed because he is considered a robber, and eaten because he is considered a delicacy.

Meadow-Lark
Early spring trailing through the meadows will bring you the cheery song of the meadow-lark: "Spring-o-the-year!" Stalk him carefully and you will find a large brown bird with yellow breast and a black crescent on his throat. The meadow-lark is about the size of a quail. He stands erect when he sings, and he has a rather long beak. The nest can be found, if you look for it, but is generally out of sight under a loosened clod of earth or tuft of grass.

Red-Winged Blackbird
The red-winged blackbird with his sweet call of "O-ka-lie," or "Ouchee-la-ree-e!" you will also find on the meadows and marshes. He builds his nest among the reeds and is one of the first of our spring birds in the north.

Song Sparrow
The little song sparrow loves the open and the hot summer sunshine. Trailing along a country road at midday, when most of the other birds are still, you will find the song sparrow sitting on a rail fence singing with undiminished enthusiasm.
To make friends with the birds provide food and water for them, then sit down and wait quietly until they appear. Let them become accustomed to seeing you sitting still every day for a while, then begin slow, careful movements, gradually becoming more natural, and in time the birds will allow you to walk among them as you please, if you are careful never to frighten them. You can do this in camp; you can do it at home if you are not living in a city. The trustful friendship of animals and birds opens a new path of happiness and one that all girls should be able, in some measure, to enjoy.

CHAPTER VII
WILD FOOD ON THE TRAIL
Edible Fruits, Nuts, Roots, and Plants

While wild foods gathered on the trail give a delightful variety to camp fare, be advised and do not gather, still less eat, them unless you are absolutely sure you know what they are and that they are not poisonous. You must be able to identify a thing with certainty before tasting in order to enjoy it in safety. It is well worth while to make a study of the wild-growing foods, but in the meantime this chapter will help you to know some of them. *The italicized names are of the things I know to be edible from personal experience.* You are probably well acquainted with the common wild fruits such as the raspberry, strawberry, blackberry, blueberry, and huckleberry, but there are varieties of these and all will bear description.

Red Raspberry

The wild berry often has a more delicious flavor and perfume than the cultivated one of the same species. Nothing can approach the wonderful and delicate flavor of the little wild strawberry, unless it is the wild red raspberry; and the fully ripe wild blackberry holds a spicy sweetness that makes the garden blackberry taste tame and flat in comparison.

The *wild red raspberry* is found in open fields and growing along fences and the sides of the road. The flowers are white and grow in loose clusters, while the berry, when fully ripe, is a deep, translucent red. The bush is shrubby, is generally about waist-high, and the stems bear small, hooked prickles. The leaves are what is called compound, being composed of three or five leaflets, usually three, which branch out from the main stem like the leaves of the rose-bush. The edges of the leaves are irregularly toothed.

The berry is cup-shaped and fits over a core which is called the receptacle, and from which it loosens when ripe to drop easily into your hand, leaving the receptacle and calyx on the stem. The sweet, far-carrying perfume of the gathered wild red raspberry will always identify it. The season for fruit is July and August.

Black Raspberry

The growth and leaves of the *wild black raspberry* are like those of the red raspberry, and it is found in the same localities. The fruit, like the other, is cup or thimble shaped and grows on a receptacle from which it loosens when fully ripe. Blackcaps, these berries are often called. They ripen in July. The berry is sometimes a little dry, but the flavor is sweet and fine.

Purple-Flowering Raspberry

The purple-flowering raspberry is acid and insipid; it can hardly be called edible, though it is not poisonous. You will find it clambering among the rocks on the mountainside and in rocky soil. The leaves are large and resemble grape leaves, while the flower is large, purplish-red in color, and grows in loose clusters.

Mountain Raspberry, Cloudberry

The usual home of the mountain raspberry, or cloudberry, is on the mountain-tops among the clouds. You will find it in the White Mountains and on the coast of Maine, and it has recently been discovered at Montauk Point, L. I. The fruit has a pleasant flavor of a honey-like sweetness. The receptacle of the berry is broad and flat, the color is yellow touched with red where exposed to the sun. It does not grow in clusters like the other raspberries, but is solitary. The leaves are roundish with from five to nine lobes, something like the leaves of the geranium. The plant grows low, is without prickles, and the solitary flowers are white. In the far north, where it is found in great profusion, the cloudberry is made into delicious jam.

Wild Strawberry

When crossing sandy knolls or open, uncultivated fields and pastures, the alluring perfume of the *wild strawberry* will sometimes lead you to the patch which shows the bright-red little berry on its low-growing plant. It is common everywhere, though it bears the name of wild Virginia strawberry. In Latin it is most appropriately called *Fragaria*, meaning fragrant. The leaves are compound with three coarsely toothed, hairy leaflets. The small white flowers grow in sparse clusters on rather long, hairy stems. They have many deep yellow stamens which are surrounded by the fine white petals. In fruiting time the leaves are often bright-red.

Low Running Blackberry

Among the mountains and hills, down in the valleys, and on the plains; straggling along roadsides, clinging to fence rails, and sprawling over rocks, you will find the wild blackberry. There are several varieties, and blackberries of some kind are common throughout the United States. The *low running blackberry* belongs to the dewberry type and bears the largest and juiciest berries. It is a trailing vine with compound leaves of from four to seven leaflets which are double-toothed. The berries are black and glossy and grow in small clusters. They are sweet and pulpy when thoroughly ripe and the best ones are those which ripen slowly under the shelter of the leaves.
Blackberries grow on a receptacle or core, but unlike the raspberry, they do not separate from it. When ripe they drop easily from the calyx carrying the receptacle with them. The flowers are small and white, and grow in clusters.

Running Swamp Blackberry

Perhaps you have seen the blackberry with fruit so small it seems only partially developed and, like myself, have hesitated to taste it, not being sure that it was a true blackberry and edible. It takes a good many of these little berries to make a mouthful, but they are harmless. They are called the *running swamp blackberry*. They ripen in August and grow in sandy places as well as in the swamps. There are three leaflets, seldom more, to the stem, which are blunt at the tip, smooth, shining, and coarsely toothed. The flowers are small and white, and the stems prickly.

High-Bush Blackberry

Throughout the northern states as far west as Iowa, Kansas, and Missouri and down to North Carolina, you may find the *high-bush blackberry*. Its stems are sometimes ten feet high; they are furrowed and thorny and the bush grows along country roads, by fences, and in the woods. The berries are sweet, but quite seedy. They grow in long, loose clusters and ripen in July.

Mountain Blackberry

There is another variety called the *mountain blackberry*. It has a spicy flavor, but the fruit is small and dry. The leaves are more elongated toward the tip than those of the others and they are finely toothed. The branches are reddish in color.

Thornless Blackberry

The sweetest of all varieties is said to be the thornless blackberry. It ripens later than the others and has no thorns. The leaves are long and narrow.

Eastern Wild Gooseberry

Among the mountains from Massachusetts to North Carolina, the eastern wild gooseberry grows. It is said that its flavor is delicious. The fruit is purplish in color and is free from all prickles. It grows on slender stems and, like the cultivated gooseberry, is tipped with the dry calyx. The leaves are small, rather round, and have three or five lobes. The flowers are greenish and insignificant. The plant is three or four feet high, with spreading branches and smooth stems.

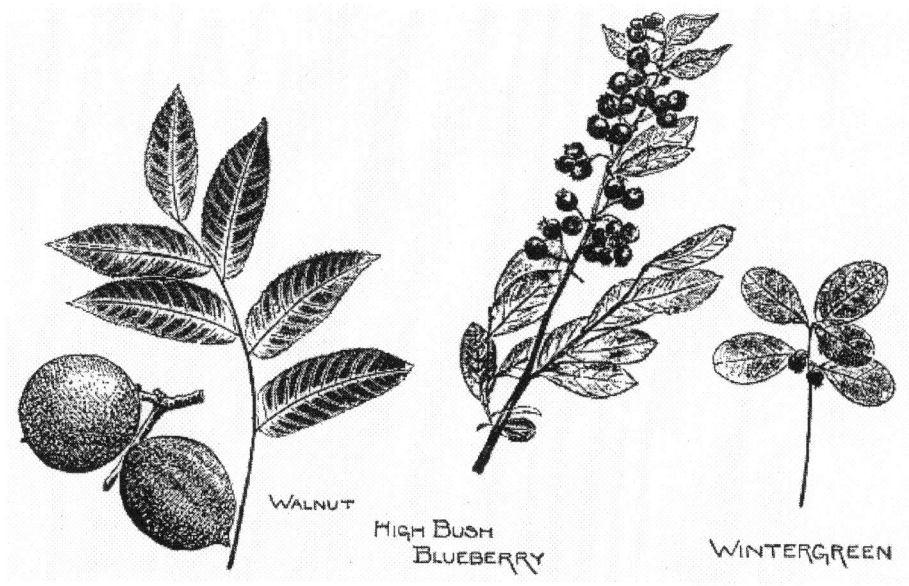

WALNUT   HIGH BUSH BLUEBERRY   WINTERGREEN

Good food on the trail.

Dwarf Blueberry
Perhaps the most satisfactory of all berries when one is really hungry is the blueberry, of which there are several varieties. The *dwarf blueberry* is probably the most common. It is the earliest of the blueberries to ripen and grows in the thin, sandy, and rocky soil which is spurned by most other plants. You will find it upon barren hillsides, in rocky fields, and in dry pine woods. The berries are round, blue, about the size of peas, and are covered with bloom like the grape. They grow in thick clusters at the end of the branch and are tipped with fine calyx teeth. The seeds are so small as to be almost unnoticed and the soft ripe berry will bruise easily. The flavor of all blueberries has a nutty quality which seems to give the berry more substance as a food. The leaf is rather narrow and pointed at each end; the under side is a lighter green than the upper and both are glossy. In the fall the leaves turn red and drop easily. The bush is low and the branches usually covered with small, white dots.

Low Blueberry
Another variety is called the *low blueberry*. It is very much like the dwarf blueberry, but the bush grows sometimes as high as four feet. It is stiff and upstanding and prefers the edge of the woods and sheltered roadsides to the dry open fields. The berries are blue with a grape-like bloom and, like the first variety, grow in thick clusters at the end of the branch. You can grab a good handful in passing, so many are there in a bunch.

High-Bush Blueberry
On the *high-bush blueberry* the color of the berries varies. Some bushes bear a black, shiny berry, others a smooth, blue, and still others blue with a bloom. The sizes differ also. The berries grow in clusters, at times on branches almost bare of leaves; some are sweet, others sour. The leaves are a pointed oval with the under side lighter in color than the upper; in

some cases the under side is hairy. The flowers are pinkish and shaped somewhat like a cylinder. The bush grows occasionally to the height of ten feet, and you will generally find it in marshy places. I know that it grows by the edge of Teedyuskung Lake in Pike County, Pa., where our summer camp is located, but it is found also in pasturelands.

Dangleberry
Another variety is called the dangleberry. The berries grow on stems in loose clusters; they are rather large, of a dark-blue color with a bloom; they ripen late and are not very plentiful. The pale-green leaves are large, white, and resinous underneath, and are oval in shape. The flowers are greenish-pink and hang like bells on slender stems.

Wintergreen. Checkerberry
Almost every one knows the little cherry-red *wintergreen berry* or *checkerberry*, and almost every one likes its sweet aromatic flavor but few would care to make a meal of it. The fruit is too dry for hearty eating and the flavor too decided. The evergreen leaves are leathery in texture and their flavor is stronger than that of the berry; they are whitish underneath and dark, glossy green above. They are oval in shape and have a few small teeth or none at all. The flowers are white, waxy, and cup-shaped; they hang like bells from their short stems. The plant grows close to the ground, generally in the woods and moist places. It is found as far north as Maine and west to Michigan.

Do not mistake the bunchberry for the wintergreen. It, too, grows low on the ground, but the bunchberries are in close clusters at the top of the small plant where the leaves radiate. The berries are bright scarlet, round and smooth, and are *not* edible. Flower and leaf resemble those of the dogwood-tree, to which family the bunchberry belongs.

Partridgeberry
Another ground berry is the partridgeberry. This may be eaten but is dry and rather tasteless. It is a red berry and grows on a slender, trailing vine. Its leaves are small and heart-shaped; some are veined with white. They are evergreen. The flowers grow in pairs and are like four-pointed stars at the ends of slender tubes. Inside they are creamy white, outside a delicate pink. The partridgeberry likes pine forests and dry woods.

June-Berry. Shadbush
There are berries on trees as well as on bushes and vines, at least they are called berries though not always resembling them.

The June-berry is a tree from ten to thirty feet in height, while its close relative, the shadbush, is a low tree and sometimes a shrub. The fruit resembles the seed-vessels of the rose; it grows in clusters and is graded in color from red to violet; it has a slight bloom and the calyx shows at the summit. It ripens in June and is said to be sweet and delicious in flavor. The oblong leaves are sharply toothed, rounded at the base and pointed at the tip. The young leaves are hairy. The flowers are white and grow in clusters.

The shadbush grows in wet places and its fruit is smaller and on shorter stems. It is also said to be more juicy. The leaves are rather woolly.

PERSIMMON

SWEET VIBURNUM

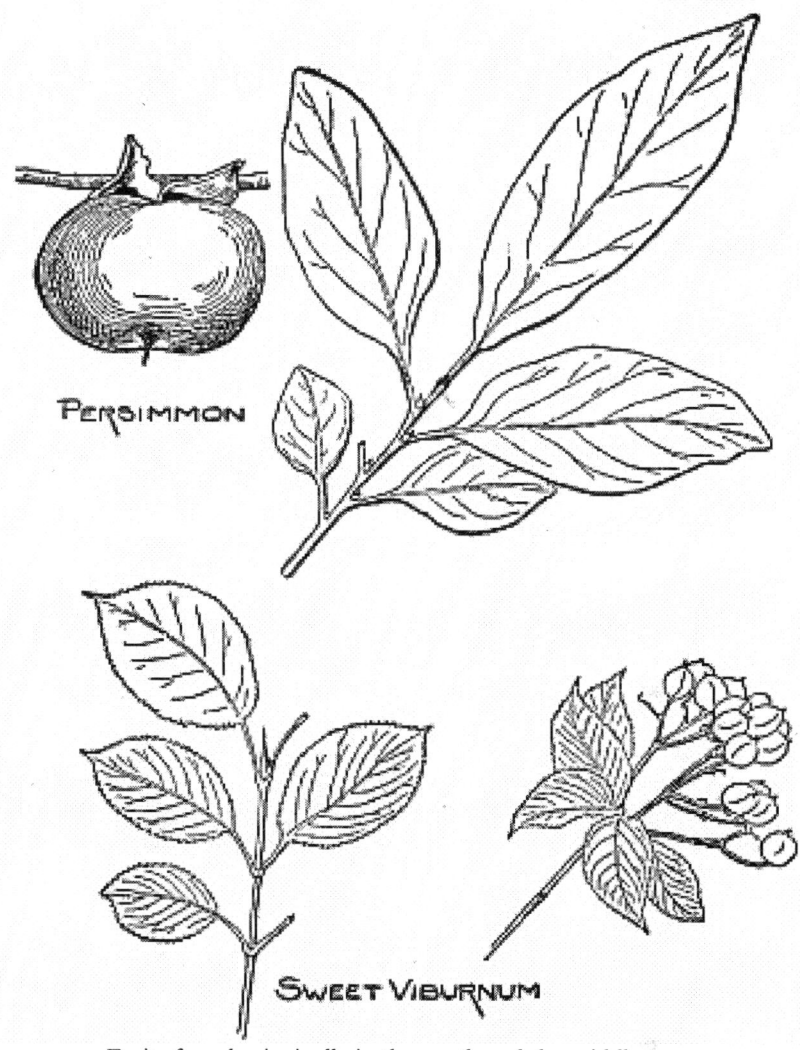

Fruits found principally in the south and the middle west.

Red Mulberry
Although the finest *mulberry-trees* are said to be found along the Mississippi and the lower Ohio Rivers, I have seen large, thrifty trees in Connecticut and on Long Island. They grow from Massachusetts to Florida and west to Nebraska. Birds are very fond of the mulberry. The first rose-breasted grosbeaks I ever saw were in a great mulberry-tree on a farm in the northern part of Connecticut. The berry is shaped much like a blackberry; it is juicy and sweet, but lacks flavor. It grows on a short stem and is about an inch in length. In July when the berry ripens it is a dark purple.

There is a decided variety in the shape of the leaves on one tree; some have seven lobes, some none at all. The edges of most are scalloped, though I have seen leaves with smooth edges.

The *white mulberry* is seldom found growing wild. The fruit is like the red mulberry but perfectly white.

Sweet Viburnum. Nanny-Berry. Sheepberry
The fruit of the sweet viburnum, nanny-berry or sheepberry, is said to be edible. It grows on a small tree, of the honeysuckle family, in the woods and by the streams from Canada to Georgia and west as far as Missouri. The tree has a rusty, scaly bark and broad, oval leaves, pointed at the tip and finely toothed. The flower clusters are large and, though white, they appear yellowish from the many yellow anthers at the centre. When entirely ripe the fruit is a dark blue or black and is covered with a bloom; before ripening it is crimson. The berry grows in clusters on slender red stems. It is elongated and rather large. At its summit is the calyx and stigma. The seed inside the berry is a stone which is flattened, blunt-pointed, and grooved. The fruit ripens in September and October.

Large-Fruited Thorn
The thorns, large-fruited and scarlet, are edible. As a child I knew the fruit as *haws* and was very fond of it. The large-fruited thorn is a low tree with branches spreading out horizontally. You will often find it in thickets. The bark is rough and the thorns on the branches are long, sharp, and of a light-brown color. In flavor the fruit is sweet and apple-like; the flesh is dry and mealy; it grows on hairy stems and the seeds are hard, rounded, and grooved. The summit is tipped with the calyx and it ripens in September. The leaves are thick, narrowed at the base, and rounded at the ends, with veins underneath that are prominent and often hairy.

Black Haw. Stag-Bush
The fruit of the black haw, or stag-bush, is not edible until after frost has touched it. It is oval, dark blue with bloom, and about half an inch long. It grows in stiff clusters on short, branching stems. The shrub, which is sometimes a small tree, is bushy and crooked, with stout and spreading branches. It is found from Connecticut to Georgia and as far west as the Indian Territory. It grows among the underbrush in forests. The bark is scaly and of a reddish-brown color, the leaves are dark green and smooth on the upper side, paler and sometimes covered with matted hair on the under side, where the veins show prominently; they are two or three inches long and generally oval in shape with no teeth. The flowers are cream-white and grow in flat-topped clusters.

Wild Plums. Canada Plum
There is a wild plum that is found in our New England States and in Canada known as the Canada plum. The plant grows along fences, in thickets, and by the side of streams. The plum is from one inch to one and a half inches long and is red or orange in color. It has a tough skin and a flat stone. The flavor is considered pleasant but the fruit is generally used for preserving. The leaves have long, sharp points at the ends and are rather heart-shaped at the base. The flowers, white in bud, change to pink when opened. They grow in thin clusters.

Beach Plum
Usually on sandy and stony beaches, though at times farther inland, you may find the beach plum. It is a low shrub and grows in clumps. The fruit is apt to be abundant and is sweet when quite ripe. This plum, also, is used for preserving. The color of the fruit is from red to red-purple, it has a bloom over it and grows on a slender stem. The thin stone is rounded on one edge, sharp on the other, and generally has pointed ends. The fruit ripens in August and September. The leaf is oval, has a sharp-pointed tip, is rounded at the base, and has fine, forward-pointed teeth. There are many white flowers which grow in clusters along the branches.

Wild Red Cherry

The wild red cherry is sour but edible; it is best used as preserves. The tree is usually small yet sometimes reaches the height of thirty feet. It is oftenest found in the woods of the north, but also grows among the mountains as far south as Tennessee. The bark is a reddish-brown and has rusty dots over it. The leaves are oblong, pointed at the tips and rather blunt at the base. They are bright green and glossy. The white flower is much like the cultivated cherry blossom but smaller; it grows in clusters. The cherries are light red and about the size of a pea.

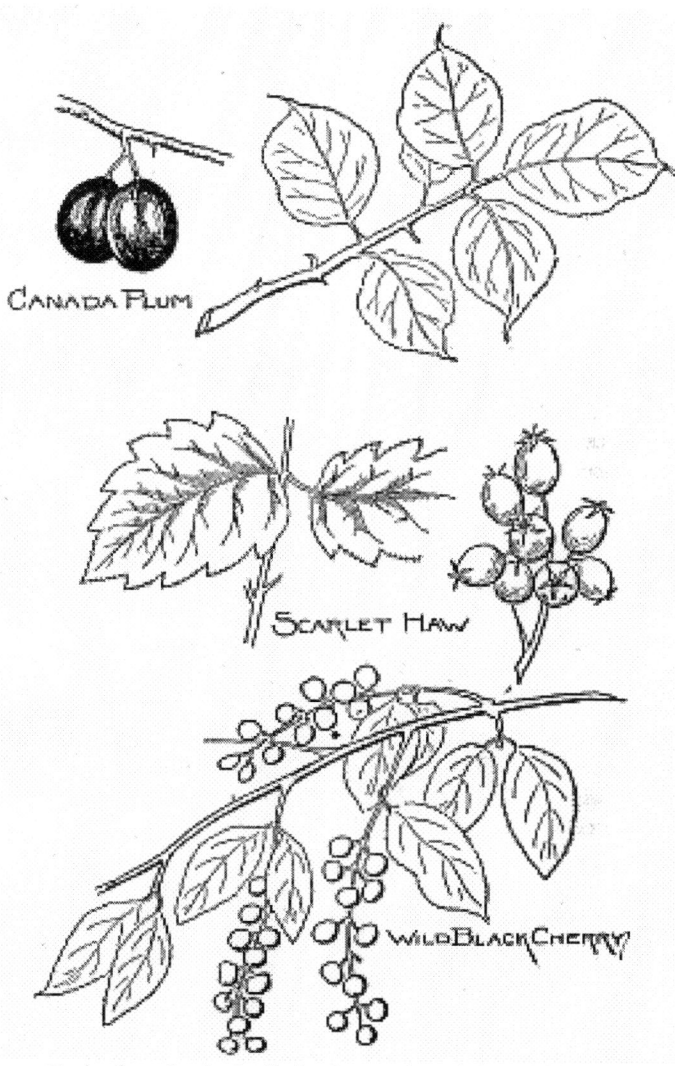

Fruits found principally in the north and the middle west.

Sand-Cherry

Growing in the sand along our eastern coast as far south as New Jersey and sometimes on the shores of the Great Lakes, the sand-cherry is found. It is a low, trailing bush, but in some cases sends up erect branches as high as four feet. The fruit is dark red—black when quite ripe—and about half an inch long. It grows in small clusters or solitary, and is said to be sweet and edible. The leaves, dark green on the upper side, are lighter underneath; they are rather narrow, broadest toward the end and tapering at the base. The edge is toothed almost to the base. The flowers are white and thinly clustered.

Persimmon
In the Southern, Western, and Middle States, some say as far north as New York, grows the *persimmon*. Deliciously sweet and spicy when frost has ripened it, very astringent until ripe. It is plentiful in Kentucky and one of my earliest memories is of going to market with my mother in the fall to buy persimmons. There I learned to avoid the fair, perfect fruit, though to all appearances it was quite ripe, and to choose that which looked bruised and broken.
The persimmon is about the size of a plum, but is flattened at the poles. It grows close to the branch and its calyx is large. The color is yellow generally flushed with red. Some writers describe it as juicy, but I would not call it that; the flesh is more like custard or soft jelly.
The tree usually varies in height from thirty to fifty feet, but in some places is said to reach one hundred or more feet. The trunk is short and the branches spread ing. In the south it often forms a thicket in uncultivated fields and along roadsides. The bark is dark brown or dark gray, the surface is scaly and divided into plates. The leaves are usually a narrow oval with smooth edges; when matured they are dark green and glossy on the upper side, underneath pale and often downy. The flower is a creamy-white or greenish-yellow.

Papaw
The papaw is another fruit I knew well as a child. It is sometimes called custard-apple because the flesh resembles soft custard. As I write I can almost taste the, to me, sickish sweetness of the fruit and feel the large, smooth, flat seeds in my mouth. In shape the papaw somewhat resembles the banana, the texture of the skin is the same, but the surface of the papaw is smoothly rounded and it is shorter and thicker than the banana, being usually from three to five inches long. It ripens in September and October. The tree is small, often a shrub, and it grows wild no farther north than western New York.
There are some cultivated papaw-trees on Long Island, but I do not think they bear fruit. Certainly none that I have seen have ever fruited. You will find the tree as far south as Florida and Texas, through the Middle States and west to Michigan and Kansas. It flourishes in the bottom lands of the Mississippi Valley and seeks the shade of the forests. The bark is dark brown with gray blotches; the leaves are large, being from two to twelve inches long and four inches wide. They are oval, pointed at the tip and narrowed at the base. When matured they are smooth, dark green on the upper side and paler beneath. At first the flower is as green as the leaves, but finally turns a deep red-purple. It grows close to the branch and is solitary.

May-Apple
One of the most delicious wild fruits we have is the *May-apple* or *mandrake*. It is finely flavored, sweet and juicy, but being a laxative one must eat of it sparingly. It is most common in the Middle States and reaches perfection in Ohio.
The plant is from twelve to eighteen inches high, and the large umbrella-like leaves are lifted on smooth, straight stems. The fruit usually grows from the fork of two leaves. It is yellow, lemon-shaped, and about the size of a plum. The flesh is like that of the plum and there are numerous seeds in fleshy seed coverings. It ripens in July and is quite soft when fully ripe. I have sometimes gathered the firm, yellow May-apples, put them away in a cool, dark, dry place to ripen, and in taking them out have found them in prime condition. They will ripen in this way without spoiling if not allowed to touch one another.
The leaves frequently measure a foot in diameter; they have from five to nine lobes, which are notched and pointed at the tips; the upper side is darker than the lower. While the fruit

of the May-apple is edible, the leaves and root are poisonous, not to the touch but to the taste. The flower is a clear white with from eight to twelve rounding petals and it generally measures about one and a half inches across. The petals expand in the morning, become erect in the afternoon, and close at night. We are told that the May-apple is a roadside plant, but I have found it only in the woods.

Wild Grapes

There are several varieties of wild grapes, all, I think, edible but not all pleasant to the taste. The fox-grape is sweet, but has a musky flavor and odor, a thick skin, and a tough pulp. The fruit ripens in September but few care to eat it. The vine grows luxuriantly and is very common. The summer grape is another tough-skinned grape.

It is not musky but is generally astringent. The vine resembles the fox-grape in growth, being strong and vigorous. The fruit of the blue grape is sour and hangs in long, heavy clusters. It is usually found along water-ways.

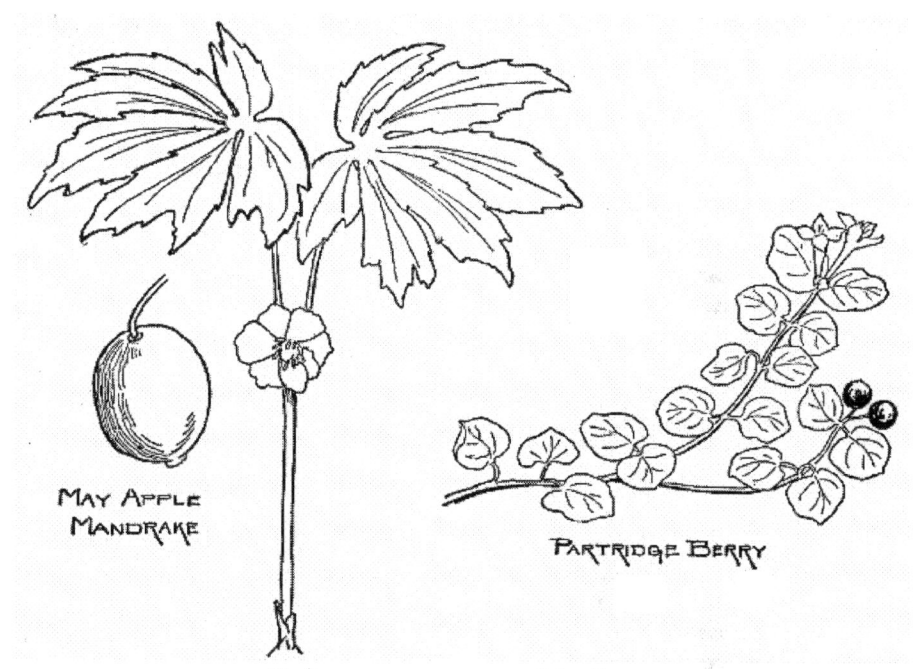

MAY APPLE MANDRAKE

PARTRIDGE BERRY

Fruits common to most of the States.

Frost-Grape or Chicken-Grape

If you try to eat the *frost-grapes* before frost you will find them decidedly sour, but after a good frost they are really fine. They have a snappy, spicy flavor all their own, and one eats them, like currants, skin and all. They are small, round, and black with a slight bloom. The clusters are well-filled and hang loosely. The vine grows luxuriantly, branching from a large trunk, and is found in wet places and on the banks of streams, though it does well in the open and in drier soil. It flourishes in New England and down to Illinois and westward to Nebraska. The leaves usually suggest three lobes but are mostly undivided. They are coarsely toothed and the under side bears occasional hairs along the veins.

Wild Nuts. Black Walnuts

Of all the wild-growing foods, nuts are, perhaps, the most nutritious. The *black walnut*, not plentiful in the Atlantic States but abundant in the Middle States and in the Mississippi

Valley, has a rich, wild flavor, and a deep-brown stain for the hands that tear it from its ball-like covering of tough, pimply green which forms the outer husk. The nut is sometimes oblong, sometimes almost round, with a deeply grooved, hard, brown shell. It grows in pairs or solitary. The tree is large, often reaching the height of one hundred feet, and its trunk is from four to six feet in diameter. The bark is dark brown with deep vertical grooves and its surface is broken with thick scales. The leaves are compound, growing on a middle stem which is sometimes two feet long. Each leaflet is a narrow oval, sharply pointed at the end, and usually about three inches long. The nuts require frost to ripen them.

Butternut
While the *butternut-tree* is much like the walnut in general appearance, it does not grow as large. The nuts are different in shape and in flavor, and the leaflets are hairy instead of smooth. The butternut does not grow as far north as the walnut, but is often found side by side with the walnut in the Middle States. The green outer covering of the nut is oblong and sticky on the surface, and, like the walnut, will stain the hands. The shell is hard, brown, oblong, and pointed at one end. It is deeply grooved. The flavor is rich but the nut being oily soon becomes rancid.

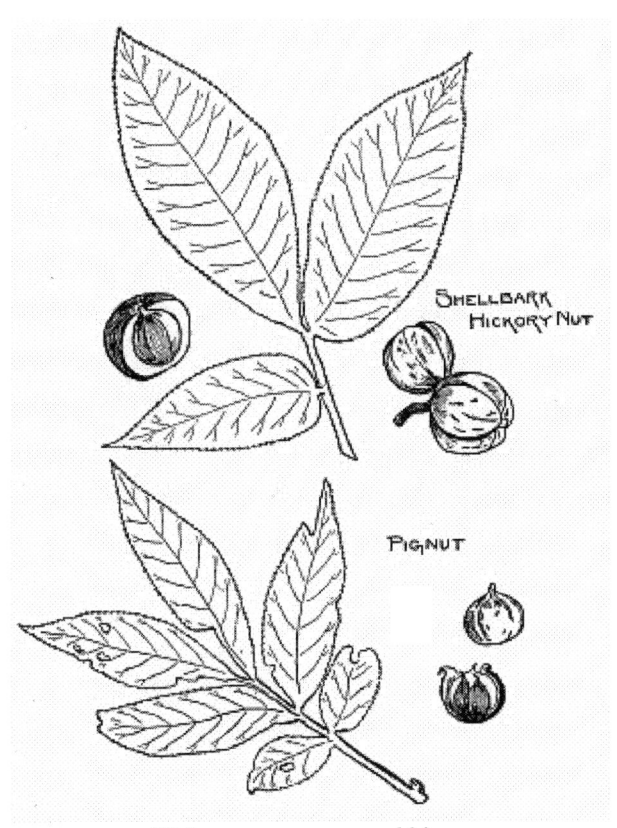

Hickory nuts, sweet and bitter.

Hickory-Nuts
In gathering hickory-nuts you must be able to distinguish between the edible variety and others that are fair on the outside but bitter within. There are nine varieties of hickory-nut trees, and in general appearance they are alike. All have compound leaves and the leaflets

are larger and fewer to the stem than the walnut, usually numbering from five to eleven. The nuts grow in small clusters as a rule, often in pairs, and the outer husk separates when ripe into four pieces, allowing the nut to drop out clean and dry. The full-grown tree is of good size and is found almost everywhere in the United States.

Shellbark. Shagbark

The *shellbark* or shagbark hickory-nut is one of the best. The flavor, as every one knows, is sweet and pleasant. It is the bark of the tree that gives it the name of shagbark, for it separates into long, ragged strips several inches wide which generally hold to the trunk at the middle and give it an unkempt, shaggy appearance.

Mockernut

The *mockernut* is the hickory-nut with a dark, brownish-colored shell, hard and thick and not easily cracked. It is called the mockernut because while the nut is large, usually larger than the shellbark, the kernel is very small and difficult to take out of the thick shell.

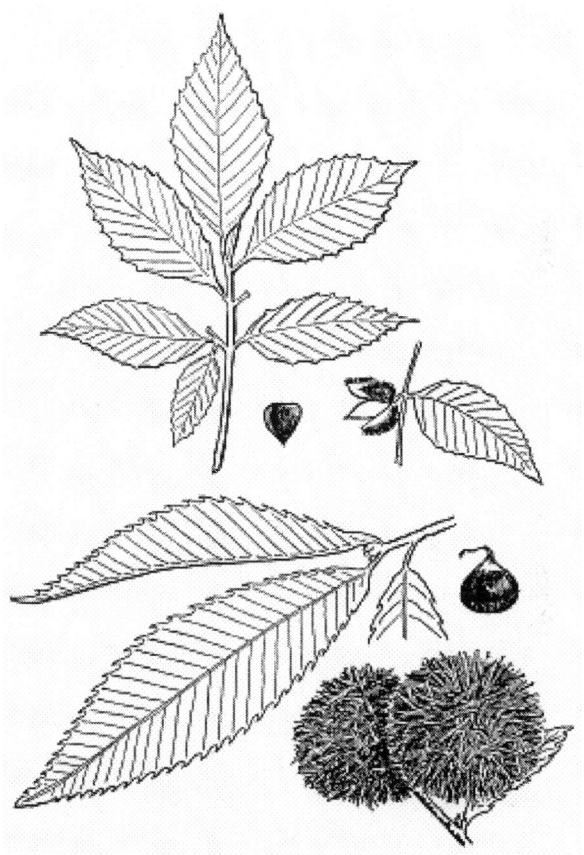

Nuts with soft shells. Beechnut and chestnut.

Pignut

I will italicize the *pignut* because, though I have never eaten it, I once tried to, and the first taste was all-sufficient. Some writers tell us that the flavor is sweet or slightly bitter. It was the decidedly bitter kind that I found lying temptingly clean and white under the tree. The thin outer husk of the pignut is not much larger than the nut. It is broader at the top than at the stem, where it narrows almost to a point. The husk does not open as freely as that of the other hickory-nuts. It is inclined to cling to the nut; in some cases it only partially opens and drops with the nut.

Beechnut
One of the sweetest and most delicately flavored of our native nuts is the little, triangular *beechnut*. The tree is common and widely distributed, but few people know anything about the nut. In Kentucky the nuts used to be plentiful, but I have seen none in New York. It is said that a beech-tree must be fully forty years old before it will bear fruit, and that may be the reason the nuts are not oftener found.

The soft-shelled nut is very small, no larger than the tip of your little finger. The color is pale brown, and it is three-sided with sharp angles. It is contained in a small, prickly husk and grows both solitary or in clusters of two or three. When touched by frost the burr opens and allows the nut to fall out while the burr remains on the tree.

The bark of the beech-tree is ashy gray, and the leaf is oblong, pointed at the tip, toothed on the edge, and strongly veined.

Chestnut
I find that the *chestnut-tree* is not as well known as its fruit, which is sold from stands on the street corners of most American cities. A round, green prickly burr is the husk of the nut, and this is lined inside with soft, white, velvety down. Nestled closely in this soft bed lie several dark-brown nuts with soft, polished shells. The first frost opens the burrs, and the sweet nuts fall to the ground.

You may recognize the tree in midsummer by its long-tasselled, cream-white blossoms, which hang in profusion from the ends of the branches. The chestnut is the only forest-tree that blossoms at that time, so you cannot mistake it. Later you will know it by the prickly green burrs, which develop quickly. The tree is large and common to most States. The leaves are from six to eight inches long; they are coarsely toothed at the edges, sharply pointed at the end, and are prominently veined on the under side. They grow mostly in tufts drooping from a common centre.

Bark and Roots of Trees

Slippery-Elm
The inner bark and the root of the *slippery-elm* are not only pleasant to the taste but are said to be nutritious. They have a glutinous quality that gives the tree its name, and the flavor is nutty and substantial.

This variety of elm is common and is found from the Saint Lawrence River to Florida. It grows to a height of sixty or seventy feet, with spreading branches which flatten at the top. The outline of the tree is much like that of a champagne-glass, wide at the top and narrow at the stem. The slippery-elm resembles the white elm, but there are differences by which you can know it. If you stroke the leaf of a white elm you will find that it is rough one way but smooth the other; stroke the leaf of the slippery-elm, and it will be rough *both* ways. The buds of the white elm are smooth, those of the slippery-elm are *hairy*. Then you cannot mistake the inner bark of the slippery-elm, which is fragrant, thick, and gummy. The outer bark is dark brown, with shallow ridges and large, loose plates. The leaves are oblong, rounded at the base, and are coarsely toothed. They are prominently veined and are dark green, paler on the under side.

Sassafras

The *sassafras* grows wild from Massachusetts to Florida, and west through the Mississippi Valley. It is generally a small tree, from thirty to fifty feet high, and is often found growing in dense thickets in uncultivated fields. The edible bark is dark red-brown. It is thick but not hard and is deeply ridged and scaled. The cracked bark is one of the characteristics of the tree; it begins to split when the tree is about three years old. The strong aromatic flavor is held by the bark, the wood, the roots, the stems, and the leaves. I have never tasted the fruit, which is berry-like, dark blue, and glossy, and is held by a thick, scarlet calyx; but the birds are fond of it.

Sassafras tea was at one time considered the best of spring medicines for purifying the blood, and the bark was brought to market cut in short lengths and tied together in bunches.

The leaves are varied; on one twig there will sometimes be three differently shaped leaves. Some will be oval, some with three lobes, and some mitten-shaped; that is, an oval leaf with a side lobe like the thumb of a mitten.

Salads. Watercress

There is no more refreshing salad than the *watercress* gathered fresh from a cool, running brook. It is a common plant, found almost anywhere in streams and brooks. Its smooth green or brownish leaves lie on the top of the water; they are compound, with from three to nine small rounded leaflets. The flavor is peppery and pungent. Watercress sandwiches are good. The white flowers are small and insignificant and grow in a small cluster at the end of the stem.

Dandelion

A salad of tender, young *dandelion* leaves is not to be despised, and the plant grows everywhere. Only the very young leaves, that come up almost white in the spring, are good. The flavor is slightly bitter with the wholesome bitterness one likes in the spring of the year. These young leaves are also good when cooked like spinach. The plant is so common it does not really call for a description, and if you know it you can skip the following:

Growing low on the ground, sometimes with leaves lying flat on the surface, the dandelion sends up a hollow, leafless stem crowned with a bright-yellow, many-petalled flower about the size of a silver fifty-cent piece. The seed head is a round ball of white down. The leaves are deeply notched, much like thistle leaves, but they have no prickles.

CHAPTER VIII
LITTLE FOES OF THE TRAILER
Poisonous Insects, Reptiles, and Plants

Insects

My first experience with wood-ticks, jiggers, and Jersey mosquitoes was during the summer we spent at Bayville, near Toms River, N. J. In many ways Bayville, with its sand, its pines, its beautiful wood roads, and rare wild flowers, is an interesting and attractive place. The salty air is fine when the thermometer is self-respecting and keeps the mercury below 90° in the shade, but the oak underbrush harbors wood-ticks, the blackberry bushes cover you with jiggers, the woods are full of deer-flies, and the vicious mosquito, whose name is Legion, is everywhere where he is not barred out.

Wood-Ticks

I had been told of the ticks that infest the forests of the South, had heard blood-curdling stories of how they sometimes bury themselves, entire, in the flesh of animals and men and have to be cut out, and my horror of them was great. In reality I found them unpleasant enough but, as far as we were concerned, comparatively harmless.

The wood-tick is a small, rather disgusting-looking creature which, in appearance and size, resembles the common bedbug. It fastens itself upon you without your knowledge and you do not feel it even when it begins to suck your blood, but something generally impels you to pass your hand over the back of your neck, or cheek, where the thing is clinging, and, feeling the lump, you pull it off and no great harm done. The tick is supposed always to bury its head in the flesh, and it is said that if the head is left in when the bug is pulled off an ugly sore will be the result. We had no experience of that kind, however, nor, in our hurry to get rid of it, did we stop to remove the bug scientifically by dropping oil on it, as Kephart advises, but just naturally and simply, also vigorously, we grasped it between thumb and forefinger and hastily plucked it off. The effect of the bite was no worse on any of our party than that of the Jersey mosquito.

Often your friends will see a tick on you and tell you of it even while they have several, all unknown to themselves, decorating their own countenance. The name by which science knows this unlovely bug is *Ixodes leech*.

Jigger. Redbug. Mite

The tiny mite called by the natives jigger and redbug is more annoying than the wood-tick, one reason being that there are so many more of him. He really does penetrate the skin, and his wanderings under the surface give one the feeling of an itching rash which covers the body. You won't see the jigger—he is too small, but if you invade his domain you will certainly feel him.

Deer-Fly

The deer-fly will bite and bite hard enough to hurt. It will drive its sharp mandibles into your skin with such force as to take out a bit of the flesh, sometimes causing the blood to flow, but the bite does not seem particularly poisonous, though you feel it at the time and it generally raises a lump on the flesh. The deer-fly belongs to the family of gadflies. It is larger than a house-fly and its wings stand out at right angles to its body. It will not trouble you much except in the woods.

Black-Fly

The Adirondack and North Woods region is not only the resort of hunters, campers, and seekers after health and pleasure, but it is also the haunt of the maddening black-fly. From early spring until the middle of July or first of August the black-fly holds the territory; then it evacuates and is seen no more until next season, when it begins a new campaign.

Under the name of buffalo-fly the black-fly is found in the west, where, on the prairies, it has been known to wage war on horses until death ensued—death of the horses, not of the fly. It is a small fly about one-sixth of an inch long, thick-bodied, and black. It is said to have broad silvery circles on its legs, but no one ever stops to look at these. Its proboscis is developed to draw blood freely, and it is always in working order.

The only virtue the black-fly seems to have is its habit of quitting operations at sundown and leaving to other tormenters the task of keeping you awake at night. When the black-fly bites you will know it, and it will leave its mark, when it does leave, which must generally be by your help, for it holds on with commendable persistence. If you would learn more of this charming insect, look for *Simulium molestum* in a book which treats the subject scientifically.

No-see-um. Punky. Midge

There is another pest of the North Woods which the guides call the no-see-um. It is a very diminutive midge resembling the mosquito in form and viciousness, but so small as to be almost invisible. Night and day are the same to the no-see-um; its warfare is continuous and its bite very annoying, but it disappears with the black-fly in July or August. By September the mountains and woods are swept clear of all these troublesome things, except at times and in some places the ever-hungry mosquito, which will linger on for a last bite in his summer feast.

The only way to relieve the irritation caused by the bites of these pests, including the mosquito, is to bathe the affected parts with camphor, alcohol, or diluted ammonia. When there are but one or two bites they may be touched with strong ammonia, but it will not do to use this too freely, as it will burn the skin.

Gnats

In the mountains of Pennsylvania the most troublesome insects I found were the tiny gnats that persist in flying into one's eyes in a very exasperating fashion. They swarm in a cloud in front of your face as you walk and make constant dashes at your eyes, although to reach their goal brings instant death.

It is not much trouble to get one of these gnats out of your eye when it once gets in. All that is necessary is to take the eyelashes of the upper eyelid between your thumb and first finger, and draw the upper eyelid down *over* the under eyelid. The under eyelashes sweep the upper lid clear, and the rush of tears that comes to the eye washes the insect out.

Bees, Wasps, and Yellow-Jackets

While honey-bees and wasps can make themselves most disagreeable when disturbed, you can usually keep away from beehives and bee-trees as well as from the great gray, papery nests of the wasp; but the hornets or yellow-jackets have an uncomfortable habit of building in low bushes and on the ground where you may literally put your foot in a hornets' nest.

They are hot-tempered little people, these same hornets, as I have reason to know. Twice I have been punished by them, and both times it was my head they attacked. Once I found them, or they found me, in a cherry-tree; and the second time we met was when I stepped in their nest hidden on the ground. Their sting is like a hot wire pressed into the flesh. When angered they will chase you and swarm around your head, stinging whenever they can; but they may be beaten off if some friendly hand will wield a towel or anything else that comes handy.

If the stings of any of these stinging insects are left in the wounds they should be taken out with a *clean* needle or *clean* knife-blade. In any case mix some mud into a paste and plaster it on the parts that have been stung. If you are in camp and have with you a can of antiphlogistine use that instead of the mud; it is at least more sightly and is equally efficient in reducing inflammation.

Various things have been devised as protection against insect torments.

One is a veil of net to be worn over the hat. You will find this described in Chapter IV under the heading of Personal Outfits.

Dopes

Then there are dopes to be rubbed over the face, neck, and hands. The three said to be the best are Nessmuk's Dope, Breck's Dope, and H. P. Wells's Bug-Juice. There is also a Rexall preparation which, I am told, is good while it stays on, but will wash off with perspiration.

Nessmuk's Dope
In giving the recipe for his dope, Nessmuk says that it produces a glaze over the skin and that in preventing insect bites he has never known it to fail. This is the dope:

Pine tar	3 oz.
Castor oil	2 oz.
Oil of pennyroyal	1 oz.

Simmer all together over a slow fire, and bottle.
This is sufficient for four persons for two weeks.

Breck's Dope

Pine tar	3 oz.
Olive (or castor oil)	2 oz.
Oil of pennyroyal	1 oz.
Citronella	1 oz.
Creosote	1 oz.
Camphor (pulverized)	1 oz.

Large tube of carbolated vaseline.

Heat the tar and oil, and add the other ingredients; simmer over slow fire until well mixed. The tar may be omitted if disliked or for ladies' use.

Breck tells us that his dope was planned to be a counter-irritant after being bitten as well as a preventer of bites.

H. P. Wells's Bug-Juice

Olive oil	½	pt.
Creosote	1	oz.
Pennyroyal	1	oz.
Camphor	1	oz.

Dissolve camphor in alcohol and mix.

Any dope must be well rubbed in on face, neck, ears, and *behind ears*, hands (on the backs), wrists, and arms; but be very careful not to get it *in your eyes*.

Smudges
Smudges are said to afford relief in camp, but my own experience has been that the insects can stand them better than I. A smudge is made by burning things that make little flame and much smoke. Dead leaves, not too dry, will make a fairly good smudge, but a better way is to burn damp cedar bark, or branches, on piles of hot coals taken from the camp-fire and kept alive at different sides of the camp.

The accounts of extreme suffering caused by insect bites come from unusually sensitive people. All people are not affected alike. Two persons from one camp will tell entirely different stories of their experience with insects. The best way to encounter these, as all other annoyances, is to protect yourself as well as you can and then, without whimpering, make the best of the situation. All the pests described will not fall upon you at once, and, taken singly or even doubly, you will manage to survive the ordeal. If the pleasure of the trail did not over-balance the pain there would be fewer campers to relate their troubles.

Snakes
The bite of a poisonous snake is by all means to be avoided, and the point is: you almost always can avoid it. With all the snakes in the United States, Doctor William T. Hornaday, director of the Zoological Park of New York City, tells us that out of seventy-five million people not more than two die each year of snake-bites.

Snakes are not man-hunters; they will not track you down; they much prefer to keep out of your way. What you have to do is to keep out of theirs. In a region where poisonous snakes abound it is well to wear khaki leggings as a protection in case you inadvertently step too near and anger the creatures, for in such cases they sometimes strike before you have time to beat a retreat. According to Doctor Hornaday, the poisonous snakes of North America are:

The rattlesnake,
Water-moccasin,
Copperhead,
Sonora coral-snake,
Harlequin snake.

BANDED RATTLESNAKE
Poisonous

WATER-MOCCASIN
Poisonous

RED-BELLIED WATER-SNAKE
Striped Lengthwise
Harmless

Poisonous and non-poisonous snakes.

Rattlesnakes

The rattlesnake appears to vary in color and markings in the different localities where it is found, and there are fourteen or fifteen varieties, but all carry the rattles, shake them warningly, and coil before they strike. The rattlesnake does not want to fight and if you keep at a safe distance it will glide off in another direction, but it is safest not to venture within striking distance, which is said to be two-thirds the length of the snake, even if the snake has not coiled, for it moves quickly and strikes like a flash.

The rattles are at the extreme end of the tail and are composed of horny joints. The sound of the rattle is much like the humming of a locust (cicada). Rattlesnakes are often found sunning themselves on large rocks, and stone-quarries are the chosen winter quarters where whole colonies assemble. They are also found, during the summer, among underbrush and in stubble-fields, where they probably go to hunt field-mice and other small mammals.

Banded Rattlesnake

The mountains of Pennsylvania are a favorite resort of the rattlesnake, but, though I have passed many sum mers in Pike County, famous for its snakes, the only live one I ever saw in that locality was in a box at Rowland station. The men of our party occasionally killed one and brought it to camp as a trophy, but one of our weekend guests spent most of his time hunting the rattler that he might take its skin back to the city, yet without success.

It is the banded rattlesnake that is usually found in Pennsylvania. The color is yellowish and it is marked with irregular, wide bands of dark brown. Sometimes the snake is almost black, and it is thought that it turns dark with age.

Diamond Rattlesnake

The rattlesnake marked in diamond patterns of gold outline on brown is of the south and is oftenest found in Florida. This is a very large snake, and closely allied to it is the Texas rattlesnake, which is the same in markings and color, but paler, as if faded out.

Massasauga

The massasauga is the rattlesnake occasionally found in the swamps from western New York to Nebraska, but it is rare. Its color is light brown with patches of dark brown its entire length.

Copperhead

The copperhead is not a rattler, though its vibrating tail amid dry leaves will sometimes hum like one. (This is also true of the blacksnake.) Its bite is very poisonous. It is found amid rocks and in the woods, and is at home from New England and the Atlantic coast west to Indiana and south to Texas. This snake is seldom more than three feet long. Its color is light reddish-brown with bands of rich chestnut which are narrow on the back and wide at the sides. The underpart is whitish with dark spots on the abdomen. The head is generally coppery in color but not always. In Texas the colors of the copperhead are stronger, the bands and head are decidedly reddish, and the bands have narrow white borders.

Harlequin Snake and Coral-Snake

The harlequin snake and the coral-snake are so similar in color and in habits, one description for both will answer our purpose. They are southern snakes, beginning in southern Indiana and extending south. They are quite poisonous, but of such retiring habits as hardly to be classed as dangerous. Most of their time is spent hidden under the sand and in the ground, but when they do come out their colors are so brilliant as not to be mistaken. On the harlequin snake the colors are bright coral-red, yellow, and black, which alternate in stripes that encircle the body. Its head is always banded with a broad yellow stripe. The coral-snake is much the same in color, and only a close observer would notice the difference. The coral-snake is also found in Arizona.

Water-Moccasin, Cottonmouth
The water-moccasin is ugly, and ugly all the way through. Its deadly viciousness is not redeemed by any outward beauty. Its average length is three and a half feet, though it is occasionally longer. Its unlovely body is thick and the color of greenish mud; the sides are paler and have wide, blackish bands. There are dark bands from the eyes to the mouth and above them there are pale streaks. The top of the head is very dark. The abdomen is yellow with splashes of brown or black. Heavy shields overhang the eyes and give a sinister expression to their angry glare. When suddenly approached the moccasin opens wide its white-lined mouth, and one then understands why it is called cottonmouth.
This snake does not coil before its strikes, but vibrates its tail slowly and watches its prey with mouth open. The moccasin is decidedly a southern snake, and girls of the south know that its home is along the edges of bayous and in the swamps. It is frequently seen with its head and a small part of its body out of water while the rest is submerged, but at times it will be found on a water-soaked log or on underbrush and low boughs of trees that overhang the water. The bite is very poisonous.

Other Snakes
There are many other snakes in the United States, but they are not venomous. Here is one thing to remember: you need never fear a snake found in this country which has *lengthwise stripes*, that is, stripes running from head to tail. Daniel C. Beard tells me that he has learned this from observation, and Raymond L. Ditmars, curator of reptiles in the New York Zoological Park, agrees with him.
While the lengthwise-striped snakes are harmless, others not striped in this way are harmless, too. The blacksnake, though he looks an ugly customer and, when cornered, will sometimes show fight, is not venomous and his bite is not deep. It is, therefore, wanton cruelty to kill every snake that crosses your path simply because it happens to be a snake. Kephart, in his book of "Camping and Woodcraft," says in regard to identifying the poisonous snake:
"The rattlesnake, copperhead, and cottonmouth are easily distinguished from all other snakes, as all three of them bear a peculiar mark, or rather a pair of marks, that no other animal possesses. This mark is the *pit*, which is a deep cavity on each side of the face between the nostrils and the eye, sinking into the upper jaw-bone."
If, when one has been bitten and the snake killed, an examination is made of its head, it can be ascertained immediately whether the snake was venomous, and in this way unnecessary fright may be avoided.

Beaded Lizard, Gila Monster
The only other venomous reptile found in the United States is the beaded lizard, called Gila monster (pronounced heela). Unless you visit the desert regions of Arizona and New Mexico, you will not be apt to run across this most interesting though poisonous reptile.
The Gila monster looks very much like a unique piece of Indian beadwork, with its fat body and stubby legs covered with bright-colored, bead-like tubercles, which form almost a Navajo pattern. Its length is about nineteen inches, and its beads are colored salmon, flesh-pink, white or yellow, and black. Though it has the appearance of being stuffed with cotton, it is really formidable and very much alive. Its jaws are strong; when it bites it holds on like a bulldog, and there is no way to force it to open its mouth except to pry the powerful jaws apart. While otherwise slow of movement, it will turn quickly from side to side, snapping viciously. The inside of the Gila's mouth is black, and when angry it opens it wide and hisses.

Treatment for Snake-Bites
If the unlikely should chance to happen and one of your party is bitten by a poisonous snake, first aid should be given *immediately*, and if a physician is within reach he should be summoned as quickly as possible. Much depends, however, upon what is done first. Any one can administer the following treatment, and it should be done without flinching, for it may mean the saving of a life:

(1) As soon as the person is bitten twist a tourniquet very tightly above the wound, that is, between the wound and the heart, to keep the poison as far as possible from entering the entire system.
(2) Slash the wound or stab it with a *clean* knife-blade and force it to bleed copiously. If there is no break in the skin or membrane of your mouth or lips and no cavity in any of your teeth, suck the wound to draw out the poison.
(3) Give a stimulant in small doses at frequent intervals to stimulate the heart and lungs and strengthen the nerves, but avoid overdoing this, for the result will be harmful.
(4) If you have with you an antivenomous serum, inject it as directed by the formula that accompanies it.

Tie a loose bandage around the affected member, a handkerchief, neck scarf, or even a rope for a tourniquet, to check circulation, as described in Chapter XII, on Accidents. Every little while loosen the tourniquet, then tighten it again, for it will not do to stop the circulation entirely.
All authorities do not advise sucking the wound, but it is generally done, for with a perfectly sound and healthy mouth there is no danger, as the poison enters the system only by contact with the blood.
Some writers advocate cauterizing the wound with a hot iron; but, whatever is done, do quickly, and *do not be afraid*. Fear is contagious and exceedingly harmful to the patient. Remember that a snake-bite is seldom fatal, and that a swollen arm or leg does not mean that the case is hopeless.

Poisonous Plants
There are two kinds of poisonous plants: those that are poison to the touch and those that are harmless unless taken inwardly. Both may be avoided when you learn to identify them.

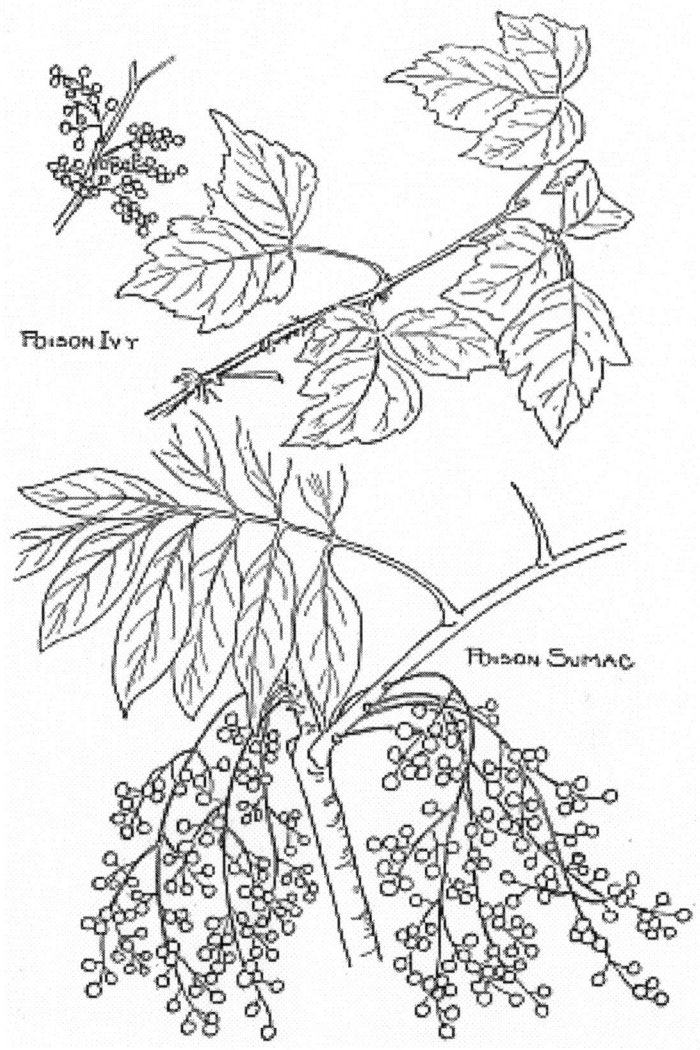

Plants poison to the touch.

Poison-Ivy

We are apt to think that every one knows the common poison-ivy, but that some people are not familiar with it was shown when one beautiful autumn day a young woman passed along our village street carrying a handful of the sprays of the vine, gathered probably because of their beautiful coloring. Noticing that she was a stranger, no doubt from the city, and realizing the danger she was running of poisoning herself or some one else, we hurriedly caught up with her and gave first aid to the ignorant in a few forceful remarks. The result was that, without a word, the young woman simply opened her hand, dropped her vines on the walk, and hurried off as if to escape a pestilence. We were left to close the incident by kicking the stuff into the street that some other equally uninformed person might not be tempted to pick it up.

If you do not know the poison-ivy, remember this: It is the *three-leaved ivy*. Its leaves always grow in triplets as shown in illustration. The leaves are smooth, but not glossy; they have no teeth but are occasionally notched. Sometimes the plant is bushy, standing a foot or two high, again it is trailing or climbing. It loves fence corners and big rocks to clamber over; it will also choose large trees for support, climbing up to their tops. The flowers are whitish and the fruit is a pretty, green-gray berry, round and smooth, which grows in scant clusters. Poison-ivy is found through the country from Maine to Texas and west to South Dakota, Utah, and Arkansas.

Some people are immune to ivy poison and, happily, I belong to the fortunate ones. Many persons are poisoned by it, however, and it may be that fear makes them more susceptible. On some the painful, burning eruption is difficult to cure.

Poison-Oak

The poison-oak closely resembles the poison-ivy, and is sometimes called by that name, but its leaves are differently shaped, being oval in outline with a few coarse, blunt teeth. They are also thicker and smaller than the ivy leaf. The poison-oak is plentiful in cool uplands and in ravines, and is general throughout the Pacific coast from Lower California and Arizona to British America.

Poison-Sumach, or Swamp-Sumach

Another member of the same family is the poison-sumach. They are all three equally poisonous and act by contact. The poison, or swamp, sumach is a high, branching shrub closely resembling the harmless species which grow on high, dry ground. The poison variety chooses low, wet places. The leaves of the poison-sumach are compound, with from seven to thirteen leaflets growing from one stem, as the leaves of the walnut-tree grow; the stalks are often of a purplish color. The leaflets are oval in shape and are pointed at the tip. The surface is smooth and green on both sides and they have no teeth. The autumn coloring is very brilliant. The flowers are whitish-green and grow in loose clusters from a stiff middle stalk at the angles of the leaves. The fruit is a gray-green berry growing in scant, drooping clusters. This *gray drooping berry is the sumac poison sign*, for the fruit of the harmless sumach is crimson and is held erect in close pyramidal clusters. Witch-hazel (Pond's Extract) is used as a remedy for all of these poisons, but it is claimed that a paste made of *cooking-soda* and water is better. Alcohol will sometimes be effective, also a strong lye made of wood-ashes. Salt and water will give relief to some. It seems to depend upon the person whether the remedy, as well as the poison, will have effect.

Yellow Lady's-Slipper

Growing in bogs and low woods from Maine to Minnesota and Washington, southward to Georgia and Missouri, there is a sweet-scented, little yellow-and-brown flower called the yellow lady's-slipper, the plant of which is said to have the same effect when handled as poison-ivy. This flower is an orchid. The stalk, from one to two feet high, bears a single blossom at the top, and the leaves, shaped and veined like those of the lily-of-the-valley, grow alternately down the stem. The plant does not branch. Like the ivy, the yellow lady's-slipper does not poison every one.

I know of no other wild plants that are poisonous to the touch; the following will poison only if taken inwardly.

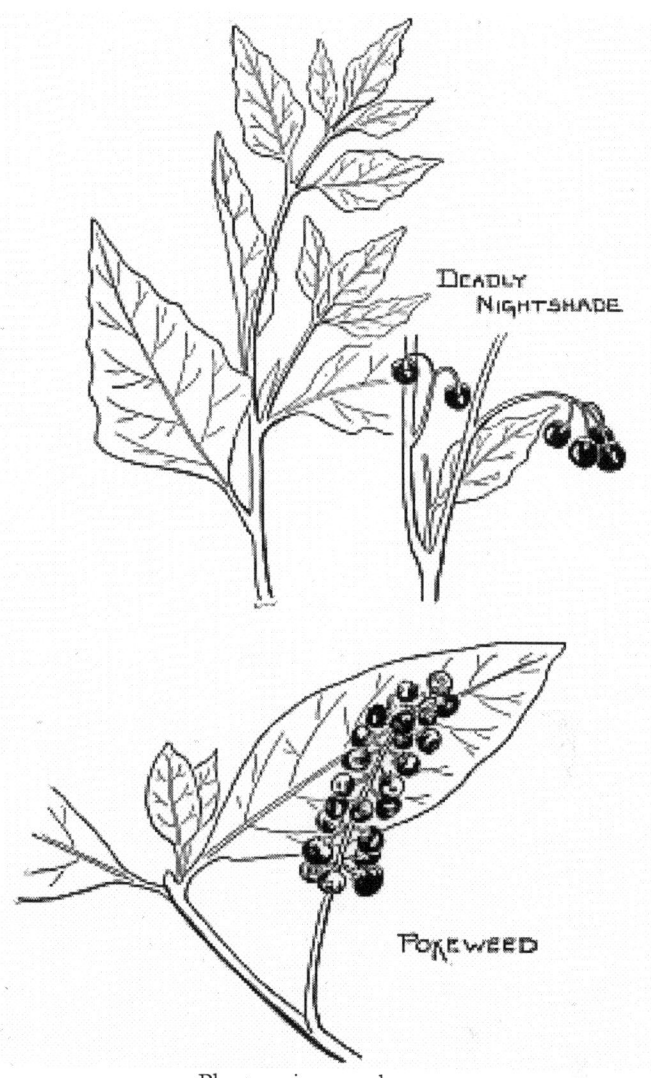

Plants poison to the taste.

Deadly Nightshade
To the nightshade family belong plants that are poisonous and plants that are not, but the thrilling name, deadly nightshade, carries with it the certainty of poison.

The plant is an annual and you may often find it growing in a neglected corner of the garden as well as in waste places. It is a tall plant; the one I remember in our own garden reached to the top of a five-foot board fence. Its leaves are rather triangular in shape, they are dark green and the wavy edges are notched rather than toothed. The flowers are white and grow in small clusters. The fruit is a berry, round, black, and smooth, with calyx adhering to it. The berry clusters grow at the end of drooping stems. This must not be mistaken for the high-bush blueberry, for to eat the fruit would be most dangerous.

The antidotes for nightshade poison are emetics, cathartics, and stimulants. The poison should be thrown off the stomach first, then strong coffee be given as a stimulant.

Pokeweed, Pigeonberry
Pokeweed comes under the heading of poisonous plants though its berries are eaten by birds, and its young shoots are said to be almost equal in flavor, and quite as wholesome, as asparagus. It seems to be the large perennial root that holds the poison, though some authorities claim that the poison permeates the entire plant to a certain extent. The root is sometimes mistaken for that of edible plants and the young leaves for those of the marsh-marigold, which are edible when cooked. It is a tall plant with a stout stem and emits a strong odor. You will find it growing by the wayside and in rocky places. The leaves are oblong and pointed at the tips and base. They have no teeth. The small white flowers are in clusters. The fruit is a small, flat, dark-purple berry, growing in long, upstanding clusters on a central stalk. The individual stem of the berry is very short. The name inkberry was given to the plant because of the strong stain of the berry juice which was sometimes used for ink. Pokeweed is at home in various states, Maine to Minnesota, Arkansas, and Florida.

Poison-Hemlock
The poison-hemlock is well known historically, being in use at the time of Socrates, and believed to have been administered to him by the Greeks. It is quite as poisonous now as in Socrates's day, and accidental poisoning has come from people eating the seeds, mistaking them for anise-seed, eating the leaves for parsley and the roots for parsnips. The plant grows from two to seven feet high; its stem is smooth and spotted or streaked with purplish-red. It has large, parsley-like leaves and pretty clusters of small, white flowers which grow, stiff-stemmed, from a common centre and blossom in July and August. When the fresh leaves are bruised they give out a distinctly mouse-like odor and they are very nauseating to the taste. Poison-hemlock is common on waysides and waste places in New York, West Virginia, Pennsylvania, New Jersey, and Ohio. It is also found in New England and Michigan, Wisconsin, Illinois, Louisiana, and California.

The treatment recommended by professionals is emetics, warmth of hands and feet, artificial respiration, and the subcutaneous injection of atropine, administered by a physician.

Water-Hemlock
Water-hemlock is similar in appearance and in effect. It is found in wet places and on the borders of swamps. The remedies are the same as for poison-hemlock.

Jimson-Weed
The jimson-weed is very common in Kentucky. I have not seen so much of it in the east and north, but it appears to grow pretty nearly over the whole United States. It is from one to five feet in height, and an ill-smelling weed, though first cousin to the beautiful, cultivated datura, which is a highly prized garden plant. The stem is smooth, green, stout, and branching. The flower is large, sometimes four inches long, and trumpet-shaped. There are several varieties of this weed; on some the flower is white, on others the five, flaring, sharp-pointed lobes are stained with lavender and magenta. The calyx is long, close-fitting, and light green. The leaves are rather large; they are angularly oval in shape and are coarsely notched. The fruit is a prickly, egg-shaped capsule which contains the seeds. It is these seeds which are sometimes eaten with serious results, and children have been poisoned by putting the flowers in their mouths.

Emetics should immediately be administered to throw the poison off the stomach, then hot, strong coffee should be given. Sometimes artificial respiration must be resorted to. In all cases of poisoning a physician should be called if possible.

The habit of chewing leaves and stems without knowing what they are should be suppressed when on the trail. It is something like going through a drug store and sampling the jars of drugs as you pass, and the danger of poisoning is almost as great.

Toadstools

Unless you are an expert in distinguishing non-poisonous mushrooms from the poison toadstool, *leave them all alone*. Many deaths occur yearly from eating toadstools which have been mistaken for the edible mushrooms.

CHAPTER IX
ON THE TRAIL WITH YOUR CAMERA
What to Photograph and How

You cannot depend entirely upon your memory to recall the sights and adventures of the trail, and will be only half-equipped if you go without a camera and note-book. Several clicks of the camera will record the principal events, while your note-book will fill in the detail.

Selecting a Camera

In selecting a camera remember that every ounce in weight counts as two when on the long trail, and that to have to carry it in your hand is most troublesome and inconvenient. The folding camera, which can be hung over your shoulder with a strap, is therefore the best; and do not try to carry plates, they are too heavy. It is of little use to consult the clerk of a photographic supply shop about the style of camera you should buy. As a rule he is not chosen for his knowledge of the goods, and his advice may be worse than none. The better plan is to secure descriptive catalogues from dealer or manufacturer before investing, and study them well. The catalogues will tell you the price, the size, the weight, and *what kind of work* each variety of camera will do, and you will learn the advantages and limitations of many before deciding upon one.

How to Know Your Camera

The camera once bought and in your hands, the next thing to do is to become thoroughly acquainted with it. With your camera you are entitled to a little book of instructions. Take your camera and the book, sit down alone, and give them your entire attention. Read the book carefully and, at the same time, carry out the instructions while the camera is unloaded, that is, without the film. If the size of the diaphragm can be changed, change it and look into the lens to see the effect; also try adjusting the shutter and watch the lens for the effect of instantaneous and time exposures. Try the focussing scale, locate some image in the finder, and practise holding the camera pressed closely against your body, pointing neither up nor down, tipping neither to one side nor the other, but aimed directly at the object you are supposed to be photographing. Then try turning the key which brings the film exposures into position.

Loading the Camera

Learn how to load and to unload, first without unrolling your film. Afterward adjust the roll in the camera and see that it is properly placed and will turn easily, before you loosen the end of the film. If you detach the gummed paper which keeps the film tightly wrapped before placing the roll in the camera, the whole film will spring loose from its spool and become light-struck before you can adjust it.

Count the Turns of the Key

With your first roll of films it is well to learn and remember the number of turns you must give the key to bring a new exposure into place. With my camera which takes a four-by-five picture, five turns of the key are necessary between the exposures. Knowing this, I count, and when the fifth turn is reached I complete it slowly, watching carefully the while for the new number to appear in the little red celluloid window. In this way, even when hurried or excited, I do not lose an exposure by turning the key once too often. Always remember to place a new exposure *directly after* taking a picture, to make sure that you will not take two on one film. In making ready for a new subject count again, for there are four things one must be sure of with most cameras before taking a photograph, and by counting you will know if any have been omitted:

(1) See that a fresh exposure is in place.
(2) See that the shutter is properly adjusted for instantaneous (or time) exposure.
(3) See that diaphragm stop is set at the proper opening for the light you will have.
(4) See that the distance is correctly focussed.

There are cameras, however, that are of universal focus and do not need adjustment. These are convenient ones for the trail, as they are always ready and can be used quickly. Being small, they are also light to carry.

Be Economical with Your Films
A very important thing to learn when taking photographs is to be economical with your films, and especially is this so when on the trail, for your supply is then necessarily limited. Merely for the sake of using the new toy, many amateurs will photograph subjects that are not of the slightest interest to any one, and very often, when a scene or object does present itself that is well worth while, all the films will have been wasted and no picture can be taken.

Plan Your Pictures to Illustrate Your Trip

The white birch-tree makes a fine background for the beaver.

It is a good idea to plan your pictures so that they will illustrate your trip from beginning to end. A snap-shot of your party starting on the trail, another of the country through which you pass, with, perhaps, one or two figures in it, and the remainder of the films used on objects of interest found on the way. If you can secure pictures of any wild animals you may see, they will make the series doubly interesting and valuable. When you go into camp a view of the camp should be included. When the pictures are printed write on the back of each what it represents, where taken, and the date; they will then be valuable data as well as trustworthy reminders.

Backgrounds

Look for the best view of a subject before using your camera; there is always a choice. One side may be much more pleasing or more characteristic than the other, or may show interesting details more plainly. If you have studied drawing you will be able also to find the view which makes the best composition. The background, too, must be considered, and the position of the sun. The simpler the background the better. Near-by foliage is not good for figures; it is too confused and the figures will mingle with it. Sometimes the adjustable portrait-lens, which can be slipped over the other, will obviate that trouble by blurring everything not in exact focus, and this lens will allow you to stand nearer the object and so make it larger on the film. It is not intended for distant views and the camera should not be more than six feet from the subject when it is used.

Quiet water makes an excellent background, also distant foliage and hills, flat fields and meadows. These may be obtained for figures, but often the very things you want to photograph most are in the woods with foliage close to and all around them; then you must simply do the best you can under the circumstances.

Color Values in Photographs

Blacktail deer snapped with a background of snow.

Another thing to remember is that, unless in broad sunlight, green will take dark and sometimes black; and brown or tan, being of the same color value in the photograph, will mingle with and often be lost in the background. If you are photographing a tawny animal, and most wild animals are tawny, try to get it when in the sunlight with a dark or flat background, or else against a background lighter in color than the animal. For instance, a red squirrel or chipmunk will be lost amid, or against, the foliage of a tree, but on a fence rail or fallen log it will stand out distinctly.

If you have a chance at a beaver it will be near the water, of course. Then the choice view will be where the water can form at least part of the background. If the shore is at the back it may be difficult when the print is made to find the beaver at all. In the interesting photograph shown here the beaver is against the light trunk of the tree which shows where he has gnawed it almost through. In all this the position of the sun must be taken into account, but the rule of always having the sun at your back, like most other rules, has its exceptions. I have found that so long as the sun lights up the object, even when from one side, I can secure a good picture; but I never allow it to strike the lens of the camera, and I make sure that the subject is not silhouetted against its background by having all the light at its back.

Photographing Wild Animals

It is not easy to photograph wild animals after you have found them, but you can do it if you are quick to see and to act and are also patient enough to wait for a good opportunity. You will often find deer feeding in sunlit places and can, if you stalk them carefully, approach near enough to get a good shot. If they happen to be in partial or light shadow, open the diaphragm of your camera at its widest stop and try for an instantaneous exposure. Very good photographs are sometimes taken by that method, and it is worth the experiment where time exposures are out of the question, as in taking moving animals. A snap-shot will be of no avail if the shadow is heavy, however, and a short time exposure may sometimes be used. Set your time lever at No. 1, which means one second, and the lever controlling the diaphragm at No. 16, and by pressing the bulb once you will have a time exposure of one second. An important thing for you to realize in taking animal photographs is the fact that though the creature may seem quite near as you see it with your natural eye, in the picture it will occupy only the relative space that it does on the finder. If it covers a quarter of the space on the finder it will cover a quarter, no more and no less, of the finished photograph.

The wonderful pictures we see of wild animals are usually the work of professionals who have especially adapted cameras; but to take the photograph oneself makes even a poor one of more value.

The skunk.

Don't get too near when you try to photograph him.

Shutter Speed

To photograph objects in rapid motion such as flying birds, the speed of your shutter must be at least one three-hundredths of a second and you must have a fast lens; but with a shutter speed of one one-hundredth I have taken very good pictures of things moving at a moderate rate. A walking or slowly running animal, for instance, can be taken with a shutter speed of one one-hundredth. You should find out the speed of the shutter when you buy your camera, then you will not throw away films on things beyond its possibilities. "You press the button and we'll do the rest" doesn't work where moving objects are concerned. Those who go a-gunning with the camera, stalk their game as carefully as any hunter with a gun, and for really good results the following method is the safest to adopt. Time and patience are required, but one does not mind giving these, the interest is so absorbing and the successful picture so well worth while.

Set Your Camera Like a Trap

The porcupine stood in the shade but the background was light.

Find the spot frequented by the animal or bird you are after, wait for it to go away of its own accord while confident and unfrightened, then set up your camera like a trap where the lens will point to the place the bird or animal will probably occupy upon its return.

If it is a nest it will be easy, for you can be sure the bird will come back there and can adjust your camera to take in the entire nest. Where there is no nest, sight your camera upon some object between which and the lens the creature must come in order to be within focus, and trample down any undergrowth that may obstruct the view. Make sure that your focus is correct for the distance and that the film will take in the whole animal. You can provide for this by staking off the probable size of the animal at the place where you expect it to stand, and then looking in the finder to see if both stakes are in focus. You will probably have to raise the camera from the ground and perhaps tip it a little. For this a low tripod is best but if you haven't that, and very likely you will not, a convenient log, stump, or stone will answer the purpose. If even these are not handy you can build up a stand of stones or small logs, or pile earth into a mound.

Whatever material you use, the stand must be made strong and firm. To have it slip or slide is to lose the picture. Make your camera perfectly secure and immovable on the stand, then tie a long cord to the release (the small lever which works the shutter). The cord must be amply long enough to reach to the ambush where you will hide while awaiting your game. The ambush may be a clump of bushes, a convenient rock, or a tree behind which you will be concealed. If there is no such cover near you can make one of brush and branches. When the cord is carried from the camera to the ambush hide the camera with leafy branches, leaving a good opening for the cord to pass through to prevent it from becoming entangled. Then hie to your cover and, with the slightly slack cord in your hand, await the coming of your game.

Taking the Picture
As the animal approaches the camera grasp your cord firmly and steady your nerves to act quickly, and when it is in focus, not before, give a quick, firm pull to the cord, releasing it immediately, and the thing is done. Don't become excited at the critical moment and make your shot too soon or jerk the cord too hard. If a bird is to be taken upon the nest and the nest is in shadow a short time exposure can be given, or a bulb exposure. For bulb exposure set the lever that controls the shutter at B (meaning bulb), and the lever controlling the diaphragm at No. 16. When the bird has settled upon its nest pull the cord, count three slowly, and release it. The shutter will remain open as long as the cord is held taut and will close when released. This method cannot be used for long time exposures. When you become more practised in the art of wild-life photography you will know how much time to allow for the exposures. There will be some failures, of course, but one good photograph among several will repay you for all your trouble and will make you keen to try again.

Photographing a woodcock from ambush.

Photographing the Trail

The country through which you pass, with a trailer in the foreground.

You can get a good picture of the trail with a snap-shot when it is in the open, but a forest trail must have time exposure. When your eyes have become accustomed to the dim light of the woods it will not seem dark, and you will be tempted to try a snap-shot because it is easier, but if you do you may certainly count that a lost film. It is not possible to hold your camera in your hands and succeed with a time exposure of over one second. The beating of your heart will jar it, a breath will make it move, so some kind of a rest must be found as when taking the animals with bulb exposure. If the light is very dim first set the lever controlling the shutter at the point T (time), then set the lever for the diaphragm at No. 16, press the bulb, and allow from fifteen to twenty seconds', or even thirty seconds', exposure.

Timing Without a Watch

You can time it without a watch by counting in this way: one-and-two-and-three-and-up to the number of seconds required. One-and is one second.

When the seconds have been counted, press the bulb again and if the camera has not moved you should have a good negative. No hard-and-fast rules can be given for this work because conditions vary; you must rely some on your judgment and learn by experience. It is said that overexposure is better than underexposure and can be handled better in developing the films, so when in doubt it is well to allow a little more time than you think should be necessary. Curious results sometimes come from underexposed films. I once had a print in outline, like a drawing, from a negative made in the Rocky Mountains. It did not look in the least like a photograph, there were no shadows, but it was a good illustration of the scene.

Photographing Flowers and Ferns

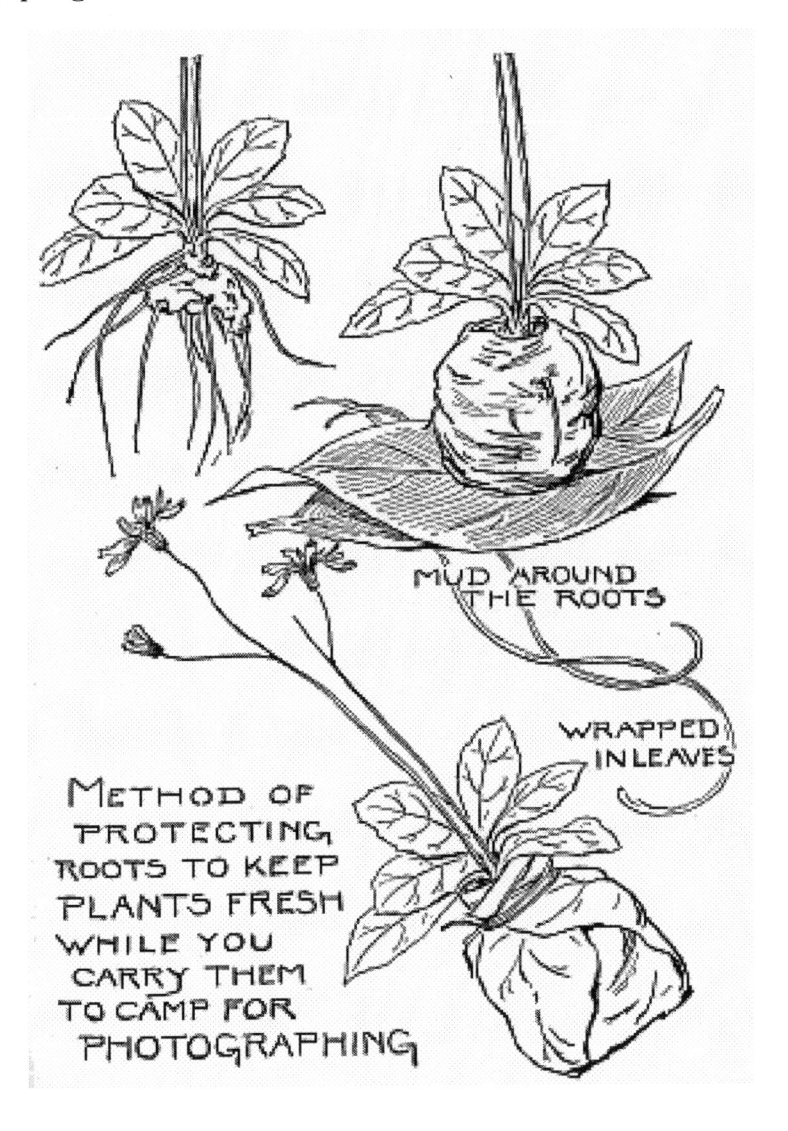

METHOD OF PROTECTING ROOTS TO KEEP PLANTS FRESH WHILE YOU CARRY THEM TO CAMP FOR PHOTOGRAPHING

MUD AROUND THE ROOTS

WRAPPED IN LEAVES

If your camera will focus so that you can place it near enough to take small objects such as flowers and ferns, another field of interest is open to you and you can add a record of those found on the trail to complete your series. A camping trip will afford better and more unhurried opportunities for photographing flowers than a one day's trail, unless you carry a box or basket with you for securing specimens that you can take back and photograph at leisure. Do not break the stems of the flowers or plants, take them roots and all. Loosen the soil all around and under the roots so that which clings to the plant may be undisturbed and taken up with it. If the soil falls away, cover the root with damp loam or mud and tie it up in a large leaf as in illustration. This method not only keeps it from wilting but will enable you to take a picture of the growing plant with all its interesting characteristics. If you put your plant with its clod of earth in a *shallow* bowl, pour in as much water as the bowl will hold, and keep it always full, it will remain fresh and vigorous a long while and may be transplanted to continue its life and growth after you have finished with it.

Just here must come the caution not to tear up wild plants by their roots unless they are to serve a real purpose. Some of our most beautiful wild flowers and rarest ferns are now in danger of being exterminated because of thoughtless and careless people who, in gathering them, will not even take the trouble to break the stems. When the roots are gone there will be no more flowers and ferns.

Look at the Date on Your Film

Even the best photographer cannot take good photographs unless he has good films. On the box of every roll of films is stamped the latest date when it may be safely developed and it is foolish to try to have a film developed after that date has passed. When you buy your films be sure they are fresh ones and that the date insures you ample time; one year ahead is none too long.

Do not open the box or take the wrappings from a roll of films until you are ready to load your camera. Then save both box and wrappings, and when your films have been exposed, use them for covering the roll again. Keep the wrapped and boxed rolls in a dark place until they can be developed. Dampness will spoil both films and plates. If you are in a damp climate, or on shipboard, keep them in a tin box, tightly closed.

CHAPTER X
ON AND IN THE WATER
Boats Safe and Unsafe. Canoeing. Rowing. Poling. Raft-Making. Swimming. Fishing

Safe and Unsafe Boats

One seldom goes on the long trail, or into camp, without encountering water, and boats of some kind must be used, generally rowboats or canoes. The safest boat on placid water is the heavy, flat-bottomed rowboat with oars secured to the oar-locks. In my younger days we owned such a boat, and no one felt in the least anxious when I would put off for hours alone on the lake at our camp in Pike County, Pa.; especially as the creaking turn of the oar-locks could easily be heard at camp loudly proclaiming that I still lived, while I enjoyed the luxury of solitary adventure. But a tub of this kind is not adapted to all waters and all purposes, and the safest boat on any water is the one best adapted to it and to the purpose for which the boat is used.

Round-bottomed boats tip easily and should, therefore, not be used when learning to row, though they are safe enough in the hands of those accustomed to their management. The best of oarsmen, however, cannot prevent her boat from capsizing if her passenger does not know how to enter or leave it, or to sit still when aboard.

A rowboat is a safer craft than a canoe.

Stepping in and out of a Boat
To step on the gunwale (the edge of the boat) will naturally tip it and most likely turn it over. One should al ways step directly into the *middle* in order to keep the boat evenly balanced, and in getting out, step *from* the middle.

Stepping on the side or the gunwale of a boat shows the ignorance of a tenderfoot. There are rowboats that are neither round-bottomed nor flat but are shaped like the boat in photograph, page 206. These are safer than the round-bottomed, but are more easily capsized than the flat-bottomed boats.

Canoes and Canoeing
If you are to own a canoe select it carefully; consult catalogues of reliable dealers, and, if possible, have an experienced and good canoeist help you choose it. The pretty canoe made of wood will answer in calm waters and wear well with careful usage, but sportsmen prefer the canvas-covered canoe, declaring it the best boat for cruising, as it is light, easy to manage, will stand rough usage, and will also carry greater loads. The best make has a frame of hardwood with cedar ribs and planking; spruce gunwales and brass bang-plates to protect the ends. This canoe is covered with strong canvas, treated with some kind of filler, and then painted and varnished. There are usually two cane seats, one at the stern, the other near the bow. These are built in. Canoes vary in the shape of the bow, some being higher than others. The high bow prevents the shipping of too much water, but will also offer resistance to the wind and so impede the progress of the boat. A medium high bow is the best.

One firm of camp-outfitters advertises a canoe called the Sponson, the name being taken from the air-chambers built along the outside rail, which are called sponsons. It is claimed that these air-chambers make it next to impossible to upset the canoe, and that even when filled with water it will support a heavy weight. Sponsons can also be purchased separately and can be adjusted to any sized canoe.

Keep your body steady.

For a novice the sponsons would seem a good thing, as they not only insure safety but, in doing away with the fear of an upset, make learning to paddle easier. Then there are the guide canoes made especially for hunting and fishing. They are strong, flat-bottomed, will carry a heavy load, are easy to paddle or pole, and will stand rough water. These canoes are good for general use on the trail.

The prices of a *good* canoe range from twenty-eight dollars to forty dollars. One may go higher, of course, but the essentials of the canoe will be no better. A lower price means, as a rule, not so good a boat.

Paddles

Girls and women generally require shorter paddles than men, as they do not have the same reach of arm, and you can take your choice of lengths. For the stern the paddle should be longer than for the bow. Paddles are made of red oak, maple, ash, spruce, and cherry. Some authorities prefer spruce for ordinary usage, but in rough water and in shooting rapids a harder wood is best. The weak part of a paddle is where the blade joins the handle, and this part should not be too slender. If you use spruce paddles keep them smooth by trimming away all roughness and keep them well shellacked, else they may become water-soaked. Paddles range in price from one dollar and fifty cents to three dollars.

Canoeing on placid waters.

Accessories

A strong, healthy girl will no more need cushions and canoe-chairs than a boy, but a back rest is not always to be despised. It is well to have a large sponge aboard for bailing and for cleaning.

At a portage or "carry," the canoe is carried overland on the shoulders, and though some guides scorn to use a carrier, others are glad of them. There are several styles, one being the neck-yoke carrier, another the pneumatic canoe-yoke. The pneumatic yoke, when not inflated with air, can be rolled into a bundle three by six inches, and when inflated it can also be used for a canoe-seat, a camp-seat, and even for a pillow. Its weight is two pounds and the catalogue price is three dollars and twenty-five cents.

Care of the Canoe

Even the strongest canoe should be well cared for. To leave it in the water for any length of time, when not in use, is to run the risk of damage and loss. A sudden storm will batter it against shore, send it adrift, or fill and sink it. A canoe should always be *lifted*, not dragged, ashore, and it should be turned upside down on the bank with a support in the middle so that it will not be strained by resting only on the ends.

Getting in the Canoe

Never allow any one to get into your canoe or to sit on it when it is out of the water. That is harder on it than many days of actual use. When you are to get aboard your canoe, bring it up broadside to the shore and put one foot exactly in the middle, then carefully place the other beside it and sit down quickly, but with care to keep your balance. If there is no one to hold the canoe for you, use your paddle to steady yourself by pushing it down to the bottom on the side away from shore. This will keep the canoe from slipping away from under you while you are stepping in. One of the first things to learn in canoeing is to preserve your balance; even a slight lurch to one side or the other must be avoided. Make every necessary movement cautiously and do not look backward unless absolutely necessary. Never attempt to change places with any one while in the canoe. If the change must be made, land and change there.

Bring your canoe up broadside to the shore.

Upset

Should there be an upset keep hold of your paddle, it will help to keep you afloat, then if you can reach your craft and hold to it without trying to climb upon it you can keep your head above water until help arrives or until you can tread water to shore. If you can swim you are comparatively safe, and a girl who goes often on the trail should, by all means, be a swimmer.

Paddling

34

36

35

How to use the paddle and a flat-bottomed rowboat.

109

Some expert canoeists strongly advise kneeling in the bottom of the canoe while paddling, for at least part of the time, but the usual method is to sit on the seats provided at bow and stern, or sit on the bottom. The kneeling paddler has her canoe in better control, and becomes more one with it than one who sits. In shooting rapids and in rough weather kneeling is the safest when one knows how to paddle in that position. It is a good thing to learn both methods.

When you paddle close one hand firmly on the end of the paddle and the other around the handle a short distance above the blade. Then, keeping your body steady, dip your paddle into the water slightly in front of you and sweep it backward and downward toward the stern, keeping it close to the canoe. You face the bow in a canoe, remember, and reach forward for your stroke. At the finish of a stroke turn the paddle edgewise and slide it out of the water. For the next stroke bring the blade forward, swinging it horizontally with the blade parallel to the water, and slide it edgewise into the water again in front of you. Fig. 34 shows the beginning of a stroke, Fig. 35 while the stroke is in progress, and Fig. 36 the ending. During the stroke bring your upper hand forward across your face or breast, and with the lower draw the blade through the water.

It is well to begin as bow paddler, for your duty there, in smooth water, is to watch for obstructions such as hidden rocks and submerged logs or snags, while the paddler at the stern must steer the canoe and keep it in a straight course.

At the beginning learn to paddle as well from one side as from the other. To be able to change sides is very restful and sometimes a quick change will prevent an accident. Like many other things, the knack of paddling will come with experience and will then require no more thought than keeping your balance on a bicycle and steering it.

Loading a Canoe

A top-heavy canoe is decidedly dangerous, that is why it is safest to sit or kneel on the bottom, and in loading your camp stuff bear the fact well in mind. Pack the load as low in the canoe as possible with the heaviest things at the bottom, but use common sense and do not put things that should be kept dry underneath where any water that is shipped will settle and soak them. Think again and put cooking utensils and lunch provender where you can reach them without unloading the canoe. The packing should be done in such a way as to cause the canoe to tip neither at one end or at the other, and certainly not to one side.

Rowing

A rowboat is a safer craft than a canoe, and rowing is not a difficult feat, but there is a difference between the rowing of a heavy flat-bottomed boat and rowing a light skiff or round-bottomed rowboat. In rowing properly one's body does most of the work and the strain comes more on the muscles of the back than on those of the arms.

In paddling you face the bow of the canoe; in rowing you are turned around and face the stern of your boat. In paddling you reach forward and draw your paddle back; in rowing you lean back and pull your oars forward. When beginning a stroke grasp the handles of your oars firmly near the ends, lean forward with arms outstretched and elbows straight, the oars slanting backward, and, by bearing down on the handles of the oars, lift the blades above the water. Then drop them in edgewise and pull, straightening your body, bending your elbows, and bringing your hands together one above the other. As you finish the stroke bear down on your oars to lift the blades out of the water again, turn your wrists to bring the flat of the blades almost parallel with the water but with the back edge lifted a little; then bend forward and, sweeping the oars backward, turning the edge down, plunge them in the water for another pull. Turning the wrists at the beginning of a stroke feathers the oar, the forward edge of which is sometimes allowed to skim lightly over the surface of the water as the oar is carried backward. In steering with the oars you pull hardest on the oar on the side *opposite* to the direction you wish to take. A little practise and all this comes easy enough.

The thing for a beginner to avoid is "catching a crab." That is, dipping the oars so lightly in the water as not to give sufficient hold, which will cause them, when pulled forward, to fly up and send the rower sprawling on her back. In dipping too deeply there is danger of losing an oar by the suction of the water. Experience will teach the proper depth for the stroke.

On some of the Adirondack lakes the round-bottomed rowboats are used almost exclusively, but the boat with a narrow, flat bottom is safer and is both light and easy to row. A cedar rowboat is the most desirable. The oars should be light for ordinary rowing yet strong enough to prevent their snapping above the blade in rough water.

Rafts

You can never tell just what will happen when you go on the long trail, that is one of its charms, nor do you know what you will be called upon to do. The girl best versed in the ways of the water as well as of the woods is surest of safety, and can be most helpful to her party. Possibly you may never be called upon to build a raft, and again an emergency may arise when a raft will not only be convenient but absolutely necessary. When such an emergency does come it is not likely that you will have anything besides the roughest of building material and no tools besides your small axe or hatchet. But with your axe you can chop off limbs of sufficient size for the raft from fallen trees, and with ropes made of the inner bark of trees you can bind your small logs together in such a way as to hold them firmly. Do not use green wood, it will not float like the dry. Logs about twelve inches in diameter are the best, but half that size will make a good raft. Six feet by twelve is a fair size. The smaller the logs the larger the raft must be in order to carry any weight, for it must cover a wider surface of water than is necessary for one made of large logs. One good-sized log will carry your weight easily, but a small one will sink beneath you.

If you have two long, strong ropes you can use them for binding the logs together; if not you must make the ropes from fibre of some kind. Daniel C. Beard in his book, "Boat-Building and Boating," tells of making a very strong rope of the inner bark of a chestnut-tree which had been killed by fire. The fibre torn off in long strips must be twisted by two persons, or one end may be tied to a branch while you twist the other. When two are twisting one person takes one end, the other takes the other end, and, standing as far apart as possible, each twists the fibre between her fingers, turning it in opposite directions until when held slack it will double on itself and make a double twist. The ends are then brought together and the rope kept from snarling until it is bent at the middle and allowed to double twist evenly all the way to the end. The fibre rope will be a little less than *half* the length of the original strands, and it should be about the size of heavy clothes-line rope. The short lengths of rope must be tied together to make two long ropes. Use the square knot in tying to make sure that it will not slip. When the knot is wet it will be quite secure.

The raft of logs.

Primitive Weaving Method

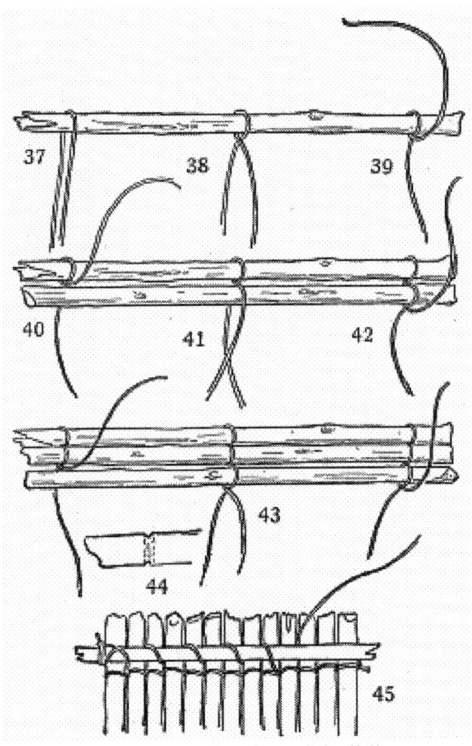

Primitive weaving in raft building.

For tying the logs together use the primitive weaving method. Lay three lengths of rope on the ground, one for the middle and one each for the ends of the logs. Roll one log along the ropes until it rests across the middle of each rope, then turn each rope over the log, forming a bight as in Fig. 37. Bring the lower rope over the upper (Fig. 38) to form a loop, and turn it back over the log (Fig. 39). This leaves the log with three loops of rope around it, one end of each rope lying on the ground, the other end turned back over the log. Now roll another log over the lower ropes up close to the first log (Fig. 40).

Bring down the upper ropes over the second log (Fig. 41), cross the lower ropes *over* the upper ones and turn them back (Fig. 42). Draw the ropes tight and push the logs as closely together as possible; unless your logs are straight there will be wide spaces between. Roll the third log over the lower ropes and make the weaving loop as with the other two, *always* crossing the lower rope *over* the upper (Fig. 43). Continue weaving in new logs until the raft is the required width, then tie the ends of the ropes around the last log. Remember to keep the ropes on the ground always in a straight line without slanting them, otherwise the sides of your raft will not be at right angles to the ends, and it will be a crazily built affair, cranky and difficult to manage.

Chop notches on the outside logs where the ropes are to pass over them, and they will keep the rope from slipping out of place (Fig. 44). Cut two, more slender, logs for the ends of the raft and lash them on across the others as in Fig. 45. The end logs should extend a little beyond each side of the raft. Fasten a rope with a strong slip knot to one end of the cross log and wrap it over the log and under the first lengthwise log, then over and under again to form a cross on top. When the rope is under the second time bring it up between the second and third log, then down between the third and fourth log, and so on to the end, when you must make a secure fastening. These cross logs give additional strength, keep the raft in shape, and prevent its shipping too much water.

If you will make a miniature raft, following these directions carefully, when the time comes for you to build a full-sized one you will be quite familiar with the method of construction and will know exactly how to go about it. For the little raft use small, straight branches about twelve inches long. Twist your slender rope of fibre if you can get it, of string if you cannot, and weave it around the sticks just as you would weave the rope around the logs, finishing off with the two end sticks for the end logs.

Poling

If you have a raft you must know how to pole it, and at times it is necessary to pole other kinds of craft. Select a straight pole of strong, green wood eight feet or more in length. The length of the pole will depend upon the depth of the water, for it must be long enough to reach bottom. Trim off all the small branches and make it as smooth as possible.

When the water is deep and calm a pole may sometimes be used as a paddle to send the raft along, but its real purpose is to push from the bottom. In poling you must necessarily stand near the edge of the raft and must therefore be careful not to lean too far over the water lest you lose your balance and fall in.

Poling is a primitive, go-as-you-please method of propelling a craft and is almost free from rules except those suggested by the common sense of the poler. Like the early pioneers, you simply do the best you can under the circumstances and are alert to take advantage of every element in your favor. Where there is a current you pole for it and then allow your raft to float with it, provided it goes in the direction you wish to take and is not too swift. In this case you use your pole for steering, which may sometimes be done from the stern, making a rudder of the pole, at others from the side, and at times reaching down to the river bed. If the current runs the wrong way be careful to keep out of it as much as possible.

Shallow water near the shore is usually the most quiet and the safest for a raft. Here you can generally pole your raft up-stream when the water is deep enough to float it and is not obstructed by rocks, logs, or snags. A raft is not safe where there is a swift current, and there should always be strong arms to manage it.

Swimming

THE FRIENDLY HAND
UNDER YOUR CHIN
WILL GIVE YOU
CONFIDENCE

LEARN TO TREAD WATER
FOR SAFETY

Learn to be at home in the water.

If you will realize that your body is buoyant, not a dead weight in the water, and that swimming should come as naturally to you as to the wild creatures, it may help you to gain the confidence so essential in learning to swim. If you are not afraid of the water you will not struggle while in it, and the air in your lungs will keep you afloat while you learn to make the movements that will carry you along. You will not sink if you are quite calm and move only your hands *under* water with a slight paddling movement. Keep in mind that every inch above water but adds so much to the weight to sink you lower. To throw up your arms is the surest way of going straight to the bottom. Do not be afraid to allow the water to come up and partially cover your chin.

All sorts of contrivances have been invented to keep a person afloat while learning to swim, but they all tend to take from, rather than to give confidence, for it is natural to depend entirely upon them and to feel helpless when they are taken away. According to my own experience the best method is to have a friend place a hand under your chin while her feet are touching bottom and to walk with you while you learn to make the swimming movements. This will keep your head above water and give you a sense of security, and you will then strike out confidently. The support rendered is so slight you learn to manage your own weight in the water almost immediately, while you have the feeling that some one upholds you, and the friendly hand may be withdrawn at intervals to allow you to try entirely alone.

You see that after all it is the *feeling* of being supported more than the actual support that counts, and if you can convince yourself that you need no support you won't need it. It is best to start by swimming *toward* land instead of away from it. To know that you are not going beyond your depth but are gaining the shore is a great help in conquering fear.

Movements in Swimming

If you are learning alone, begin in quiet, shallow water only deep enough to float you; waist-high is sufficiently deep. Assume the first position for swimming by throwing your body forward with arms extended and palms of hands together, at the same time lifting your feet from the bottom with a spring. This should bring your body out perfectly straight in the water, feet together and arms ready for the first movement.

Now separate your hands, turn them palm outward, and swing your arms around in a half-circle until they extend straight out from the sides, pushing the water back with your hands. In the second movement bend your elbows and bring them down with palms of hands together under your chin, and at the same time draw your legs up under your body with knees and feet still held close together. The third movement is to send your arms shooting straight ahead, while your legs, separating, describe a half-circle and your feet pushing against the water force you forward and then come together again in the first position.

This is a point to be remembered: always thrust your hands forward, to open the way, and your feet back, to push yourself through it, at the *same time*. It is like a wire spring being freed at both ends at once, each end springing away from the middle.

When you push the spring together, that is, when in taking the second movement you draw in your hands and feet, do it slowly; then take the third movement—letting the spring out—quickly, thrusting out your hands in front and your feet at the back with a sudden movement, pushing your feet strongly against the water and stretching yourself out as far as you can reach.

Floating

Some people can float who cannot swim. Others can swim but are not able to float. That is, they think they are not and do not seem willing to try, but it is quite necessary every one should know how to rest in the water, and learning to float is very essential.

The hand of a friend will help you in this as in learning to swim, but for floating it is held under the back of your head instead of under your chin. Lie on your back with legs straight before you, feet together, arms close at your sides, and head thrown back; trust the water to bear you up and all that is necessary to keep you afloat is a rotary motion of your hands *under* water. After a time all movement may be given up and you will lie easily and quietly as on a bed. It is said that it is easier for women and girls to float than for men, because their bones are lighter, and some learn to float the first time they enter the water; all of which is very encouraging to girls. Breathe deeply but naturally while floating, for the more air there is in your lungs the more buoyant will be your body and the higher it will float. If your body is inclined to roll from side to side spread out your arms *under* water until you steady yourself. If your feet persist in sinking extend your arms above your head *under* water and this will maintain the balance.

Do not try to lift your head, but keep it well back in the water. If your nose and mouth are out that is all that is necessary. Let your muscles relax and lie limply.

To regain your feet after floating bring your arms in front and pull on the water with scooped hands while raising your body from the hips.

Diving

You will learn to dive merely for the joy of the quick plunge into cool waters, but there are times when to understand diving may mean the saving of your own or some one else's life, and no matter how suddenly or unexpectedly you are cast into the water by accident, you will retain your self-possession and be able to strike out and swim immediately.

One should never dive into unknown water if it can be avoided, but as on the trail all water is likely to be unknown, investigate it well before diving and look out for hidden rocks. Do not dive into shallow water; that is dangerous. If you are to dive from the bank some distance above the water, stand on the edge with your toes reaching over it. Extend your arms, raise them, and duck your head between with your arms, forming an arch above, your ears covered by your arms. Lock your thumbs together to keep your hands from separating when they strike the water. Bend your knees slightly and spring from them, but straighten them immediately so that you will be stretched full length as you enter the water. As soon as your body is in the water curve your back inward, lift your head up, and make a curve through the water to the surface.

Breathing

Breathe through your nose always when swimming as well as when walking. To open your mouth while swimming is usually to swallow a pint or two of water. Exhale your breath as you thrust your hands forward, inhale it as you bring them back. "Blow your hands from you."

Treading Water

In treading water you maintain an upright position as in walking. Some one says: "To tread water is like running up-stairs rapidly." Try running up-stairs and you will get the leg movement. While the water is up to your neck, bend your elbows and bring your hands to the surface, then keep the palms pressing down the water. The principle is the same as in swimming. When you swim you force the water back with your hands and feet and so send your body forward. When you tread water you force the water *down* with your hands and feet and so send your body, or keep it, up.

It is even possible to stand quite still in deep water when you learn to keep your balance. All you do is to spread out your arms at the sides on a line with your shoulders and keep your head well back. You may go below the surface once or twice until you learn, but you will come up again and the feat is well worth while. What an outdoor girl should strive for is to become thoroughly at home in the water so that she may enter it fearlessly and know what to do when she is there.

For dinner.

Fishing

Just here would seem to be the place to talk of fishing, but I am not going to try to tell you how to fish; that would take a volume, there are so many kinds of fish and so many ways of fishing. One way is to cut a slender pole, tie a fish-line on the small end, tie a fish-hook to the end of the line, bait it with an angleworm, stand on the bank, drop the hook and bait into the water, and await results. Another way is to put together a delicate, quivering fishing-rod, carefully select a "fly," adjust it, stand on the bank, or in a boat, and "cast" the fly far out on the water with a dexterous turn of the wrist. You may catch fish in either way, but in some cases the pole and angleworm is the surest.

The veteran.

A visitor stood on the bank of our Pike County lake and skilfully sent his fly skimming over the water while the boy of the family, catching perch with his home-cut pole and angleworms, was told to watch and learn. He did watch politely for a while, then turned again to his own affairs. Once more some one said: "Look at Mr. J., boy, and learn to cast a fly." But the boy, placidly fishing, returned: "I'd rather know how to catch fish." It was true the boy had caught the fish and the skilful angler had not. All of which goes to prove that if it is fish you want, just any kind of fish and not the excitement of the sport, a pole like the boy's will probably be equal to all requirements. But there are black bass in the lake, and had one of them been in that particular part of it, no doubt the fly would have tempted him, and the experience and skill of Mr. J. supplemented by his long, flexible rod, his reel and landing net, would have done the rest, while the boy had little chance of such a bite and almost none of landing a game fish like the bass.

If you want to fish, and every girl on the trail should know how, take it up in a common-sense way and learn from an experienced person. Own a good, serviceable rod and fishing tackle and let it be your business to know why they are good. Make up your mind to long, patient, trying waits, to early and late excursions, and to some disappointments. Take a fisherman's luck cheerfully and carry the thing through like a true sportsman.

There is one thing to remember which sportsmen sometimes forget in the excitement of the game and that is *not to catch more fish than you have use for*. One need not be cruel even to cold-blooded fish, nor need one selfishly grab all one can get merely for the sake of the getting and without a thought for those who are to come after. We have all heard of good fishing places which have been "fished out," and that could not be if the fishermen had taken only as many as they could use. This rule holds good all through the wild: Take what you need, it is yours, but all the rest belongs to others.

CHAPTER XI
USEFUL KNOTS AND HOW TO TIE THEM
Square Knots. Hitching Knots. Other Knots

Every outdoor girl should know what knots to use for various purposes and how to tie them, but only those which will be found useful on the trail are given here.

Terms Used in Knot-Tying

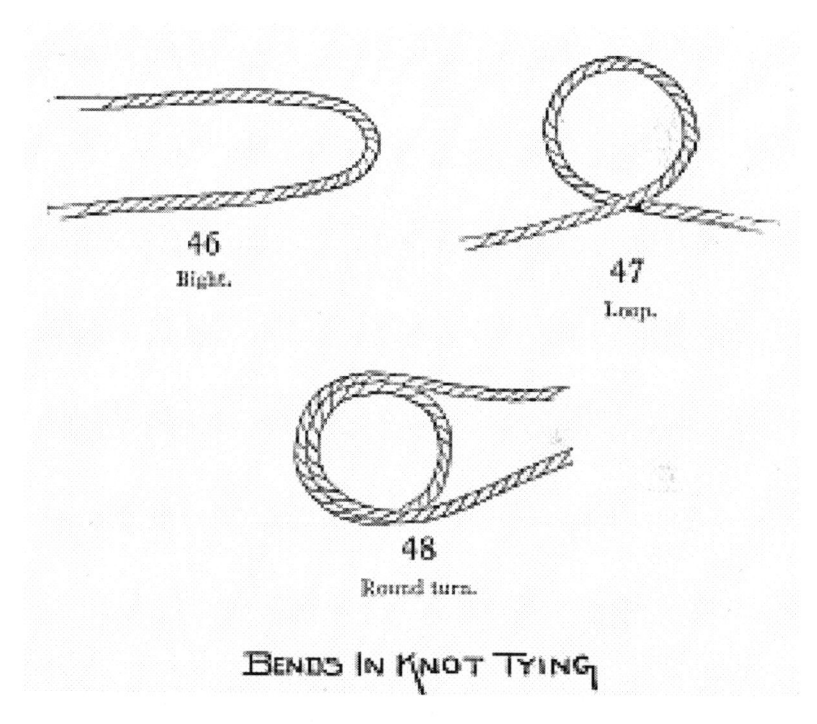

46
Bight.

47
Loop.

48
Round turn.

BENDS IN KNOT TYING

There are three different kinds of bends that are given a rope in the process of tying a knot, and each bend has its own name. You must learn these in order to understand the directions for knot-tying; they are: the *bight*, the *loop*, and the *round turn*.

The *bight* (Fig. 46) is made by bending the rope so that the sides are parallel. The *loop* (Fig. 47) is made by lapping one rope of the bight across the other. The *round turn* (Fig. 48) is made by carrying one rope of the loop all the way around to the other side, making half of the loop double.

Square Knot

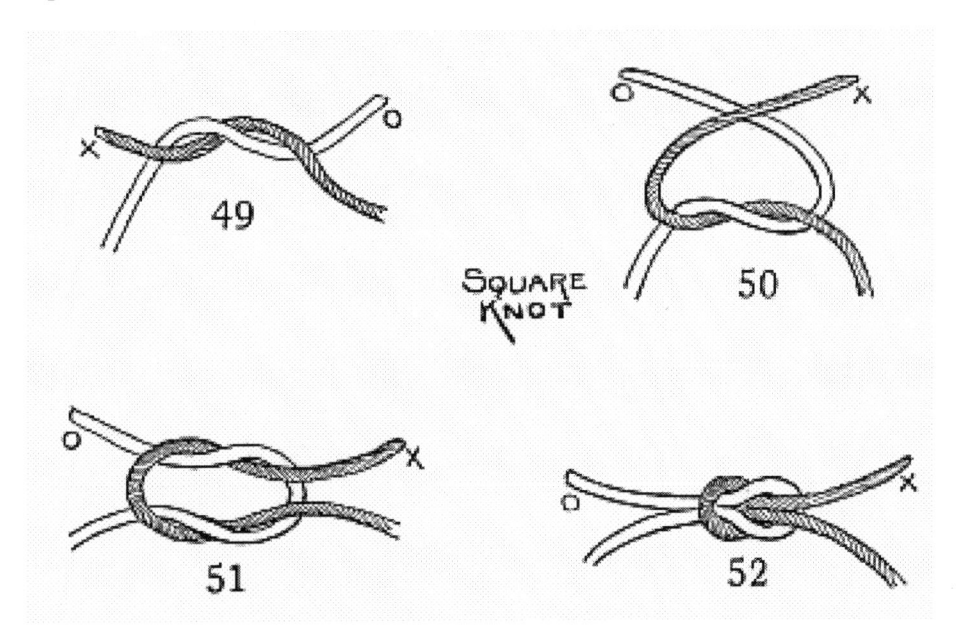

Figures 49, 50, 51, 52 — Square Knot

This is probably what you would at first call a hard knot, and so it is a hard knot to come untied of itself or to slip, but it is easy to untie when necessary. The hard knot most people tie is not quite the same as the square knot, though it does resemble it.

The ordinary hard knot is what is known as the *granny* knot, a slurring name which means a failure. The granny knot will not always stay tied, it often slips and it cannot be trusted when absolute security is needed.

Begin the *square knot* with the single first tie (Fig. 49). You see the end X turns up *over* the other rope while the end O laps *under* the rope. Now bring the two ends together, lapping X over O (Fig. 50). Then pass X back under O, making the single tie once more. Now compare what you have done with Fig. 51. Notice in the drawing that the ends of rope X are *both over* the right-hand bight, and the ends of rope O are *both under* the left-hand bight. Draw the square knot tight and it looks like Fig. 52

You cannot make a mistake in tying the square knot if you remember to notice which end is on top, or laps *over* the other rope when the first single tie is made (Fig. 49), and then be sure to lap this *same end over* the other end in making the second tie which finishes the knot.

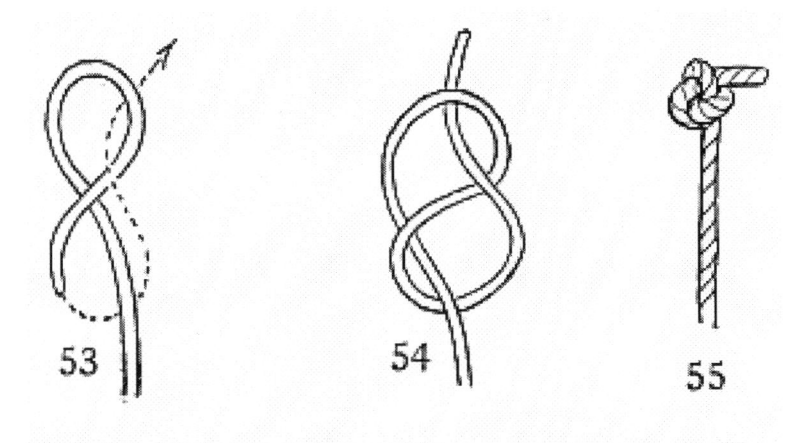

Figure Eight Knot

Figure-Eight Knot

Use the figure-eight knot to make a knot on the end of a rope or to prevent the end of the strands from untwisting. Form a loop like Fig. 53 near the end of the rope, bringing the short end over the long rope; then pass the short end under the long rope once, as shown by dotted line, and carry it up over and through the loop (Fig. 54). Pull it up tightly to bring the end square across the rope (Fig. 53). This knot is not difficult to untie.

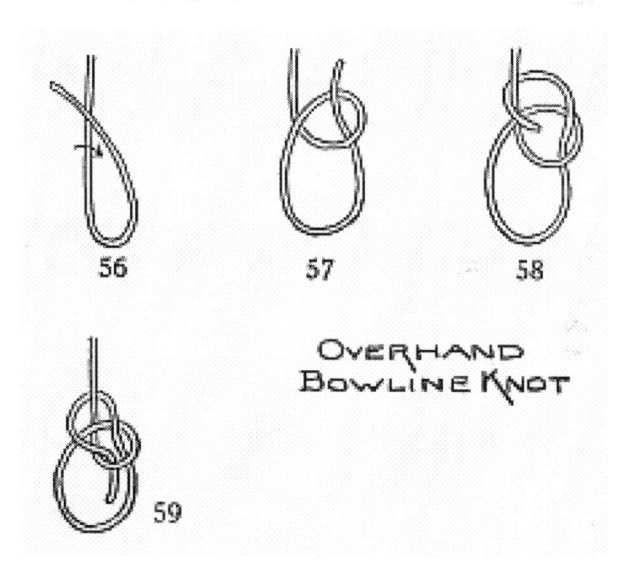

Overhand Bowline Knot

Bow-Line Knot

To form a loop that will not slip and yet may be easily untied use the bow-line knot.
(1) When the loop is not fastened to anything use the *overhand method* of tying it. First measure off sufficient rope for the loop you wish to make and hold the place with your left hand (this place is indicated by the arrow in Fig. 56); then with your right hand throw the short end of the rope over the long rope (Fig. 56). Still holding the short end with your right hand, with the left hand bring the long rope up to form a loop over the end (Fig. 54).

121

Now with your right hand take up the end, draw it farther through the loop, and pass it behind the long rope above the loop, from right to left (Fig. 58). Bring the end forward again and slip it downward through the loop (Fig. 59). Draw the knot tight and it cannot slip, no matter how great the strain.

(2) Use the *underhand method* when the loop is passed *around* something or *through* a ring. This loop may be put around the neck of a horse or cow without danger of injury, for it will not slip and tighten. It can also be used in place of the hitching tie.

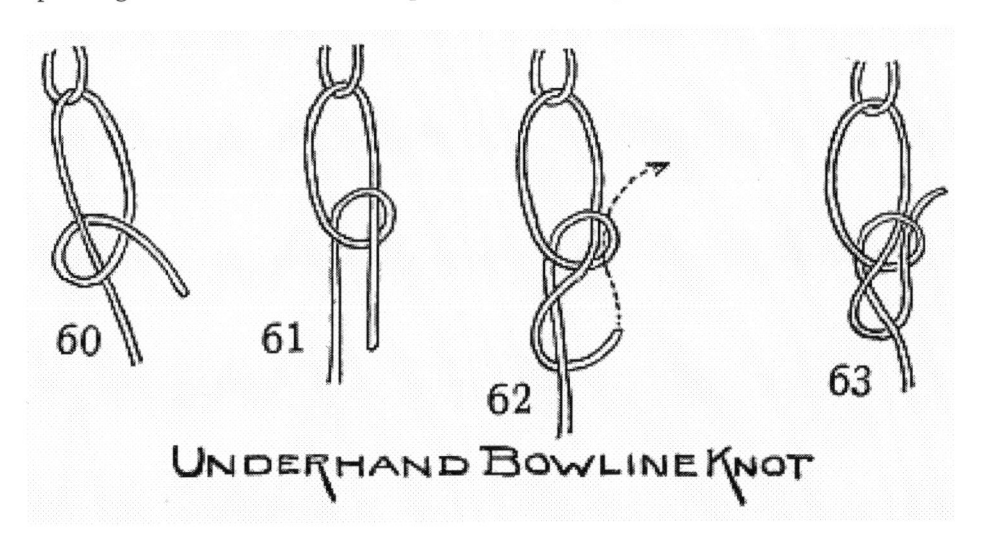

UNDERHAND BOWLINE KNOT

Slip the rope through the ring, or around the object, from left to right while you hold the long rope in your left hand. Take a half-hitch around the long rope, passing the end *over* the long rope, then under it. This makes a loop like Fig. 60. Transfer this loop from the short rope to the long rope by holding loosely, or giving slack, with the left hand and pulling up with the right. A little practise will enable you to do this easily. Fig. 61 shows the loop transferred to the long rope with the short end passing through it. At this stage carry the short end over, then under the long rope *below* the loop (Fig. 62), then up and through the loop as in Fig. 63. Tighten the knot by pulling on both the long rope and the short end.

Fig 64
SHEEPSHANK KNOT

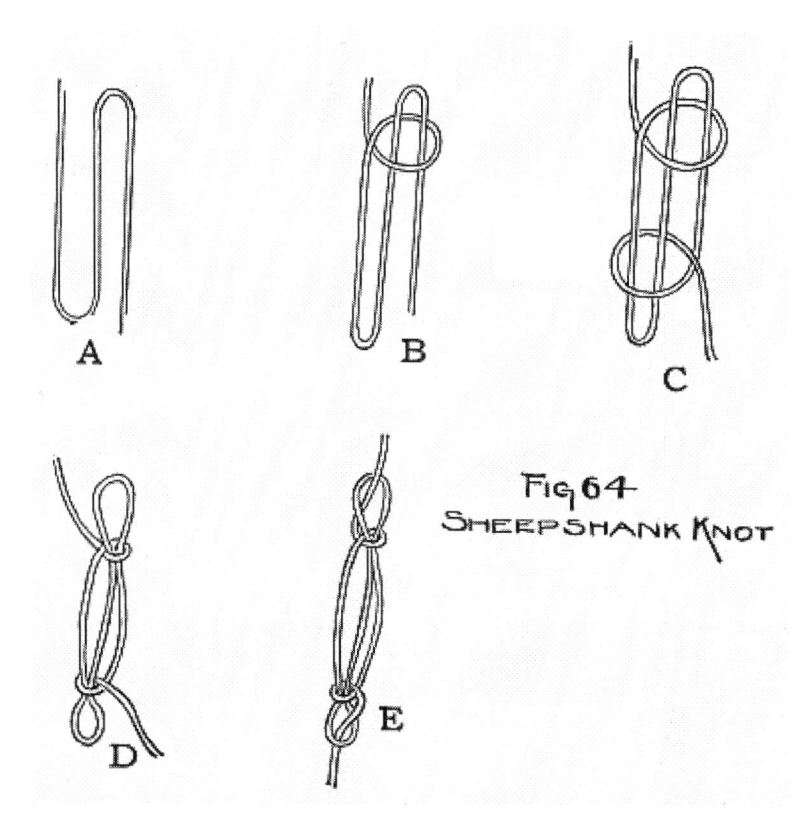

Sheep-Shank Knot

It is sometimes necessary to shorten a rope temporarily and not desirable to cut it, and the sheep-shank knot solves the problem. It is used by the sailors, who do not believe in cutting ropes. It will stand a tremendous strain without slipping, but will loosen when held slack, and can be untied by a quick jerk of the two outside ropes forming the bights.

Begin by bending the rope to form two bights as in *A*, Fig. 64, carry the single rope over at the top of the bend, then under to form a half-hitch as in *B*. Do the same with the other single rope at the bottom of the bend *C*, and draw both ends tight (*D*). With a little practise this can be done very quickly. If the rope is to be permanently shortened pass the ends through the first and second bights at the bend as in *E*, and the knot will hold for any length of time.

Fig 65 Parcel Slipknot

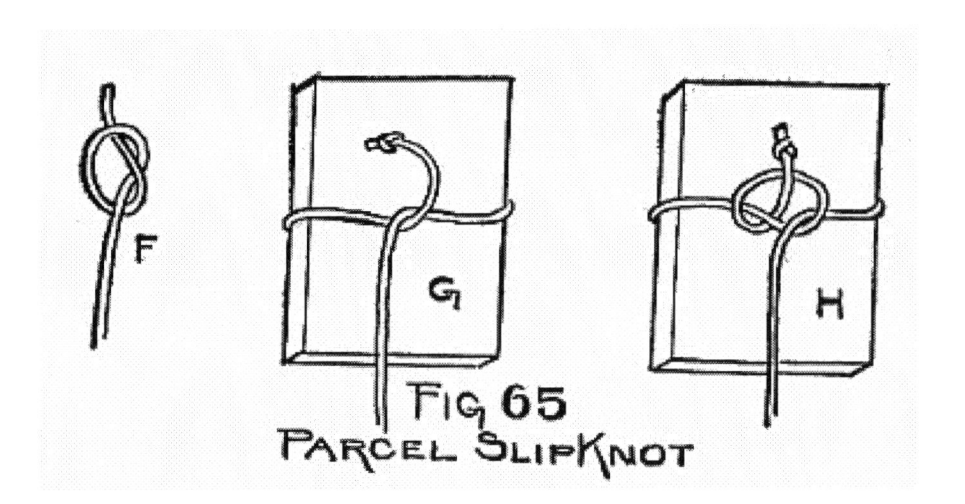

The Parcel Slip-Knot
This is the simplest of all knots to start with in tying up a parcel. Begin by making a knot about one inch from the end of your twine, using the single tie like F (Fig. 65). If this does not make the knot large enough use the figure-eight knot. The single tie is sufficient in ordinary cases. Wrap your twine once around your parcel, lapping the long twine over the knotted end as in G. Bring the knotted end over the long twine, forming a bight, then *over* and *under* its own twine with the single tie (H). Draw the tie up close to the knot at the end; the knot prevents it from slipping off. Now the long twine may be drawn tight or loosened at will, and will hold the first wrap in place while the twine is being wrapped around the package in a different place.

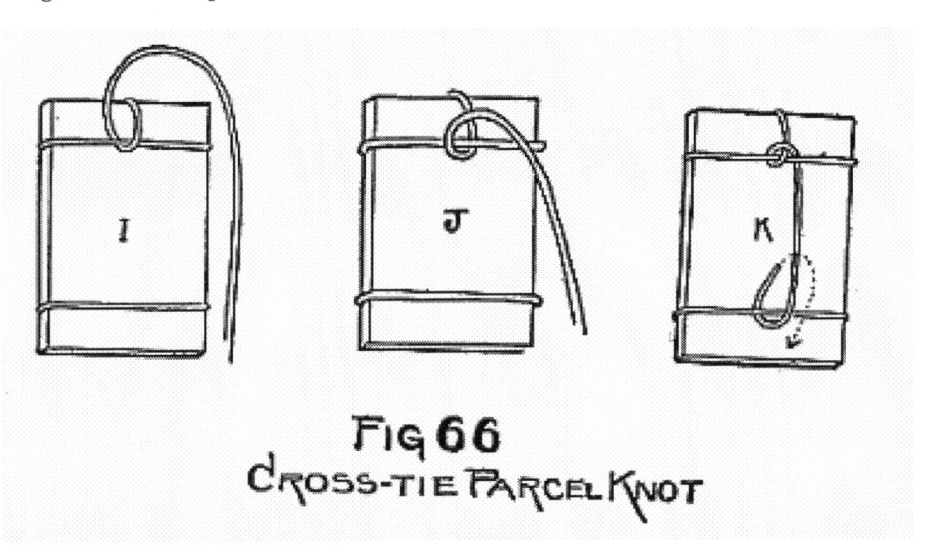

Fig 66 Cross-Tie Parcel Knot

Cross-Tie Parcel Knot
When you have two or more parallel twines on your parcel and have begun to bring down the cross-line, secure it to each twine in this way: Bring the long twine down and loop it under the first twine to form a bight as in I (Fig. 66).
Then carry the long twine over, itself forming a loop (J), then under the first twine as in K. Draw tight and proceed to the second twine, making the same cross-tie.

When you have carried your cross-line entirely around the parcel, tie it securely to the first twine where it began and finish with a single-tie knot, making a knot on the last end of the twine close to the fastening, to keep the end from slipping through.

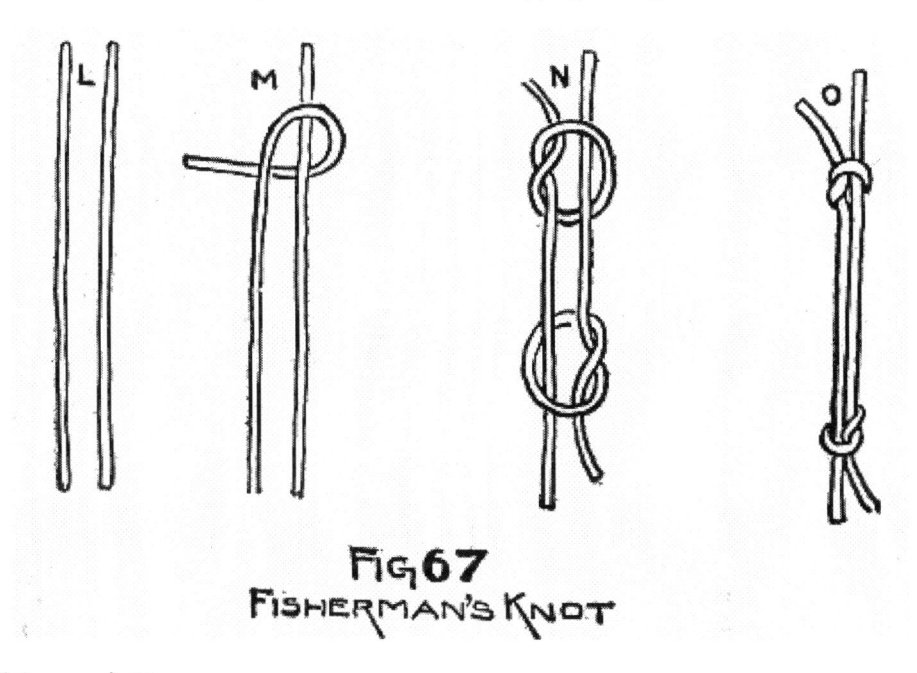

FIG 67
FISHERMAN'S KNOT

Fisherman's Knot

The fisherman's knot is used by fishermen to tie silkworm gut together. It is easily untied by pulling the two short ends, but it never slips. Lay the two ropes side by side (*L*, Fig. 67), then make a loop around one rope with the other rope, passing the end under both ropes (*M*). Bring the end over and into the loop to make a single tie (*N*). Tie the end of the second rope around the first rope in the same manner (*N*) and draw both knots tight (*O*).

Halter, Slip, or Running Knot

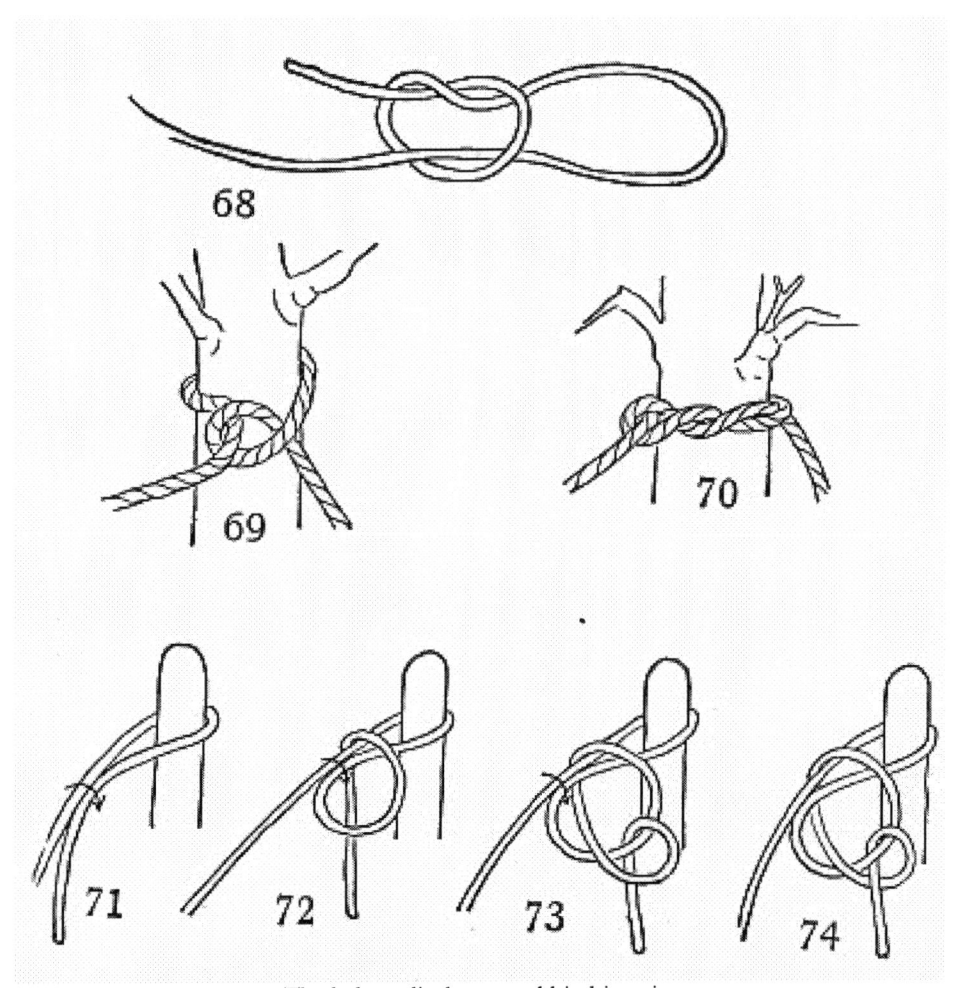

The halter, slip-knot, and hitching-tie.

The halter or slip knot is often convenient, but should never be used around the neck of an animal, for if either end is pulled it will slip and tighten, thereby strangling the creature.
First form a bight, then with one end of the rope make a single tie around the other rope (Fig. 68).

Half-Hitch
If you have anything to do with horses or boats you must know how to make the proper ties for hitching the horse to a post, or a boat to a tree, stump, or anything else that is handy. The half-hitch is a loop around a rope with the short end secured under the loop (Fig. 69). This answers for a temporary, but not a secure, fastening.

Timber-Hitch
When you want a temporary fastening, secure yet easily undone, make a *timber-hitch* (Fig. 70). Pass the rope around an object, take a half-hitch around the rope, and pass the short end once more between the rope and the object.

Hitching Tie
If the hitching tie is properly made, and the knot turned to the *right* of the post, the stronger the pull on the long end of the rope, the tighter the hold, and the loop will not slip down even on a smooth, plain post. If the knot is turned to the left, or is directly in front, the loop will not pull tight and will slide down. For the reason that the loop will tighten, the *hitching tie* should never be used around the neck of a horse, as it might pull tight and the animal be strangled.

In making the hitching tie, first pass the rope from left to right around the post, tree, or stump; bring it together and hold in the left hand. The left hand is represented by the arrow (Fig. 71). With the right hand throw the short end of the rope across the ropes in front of the left hand, forming a loop below the left hand (Fig. 72). Slip the right hand through this loop, grasp the rope just in front, and pull it back to form a bight, as you make a chain-stitch in crocheting (Fig. 73). Down through this last bight pass the end of the rope and pull the knot tight (Fig. 74).

CHAPTER XII
ACCIDENTS
Sprains. Bruises. Burns. Cuts. Sunstroke. Drowning

One learns quickly how to take care of oneself while on the trail, and serious accidents seldom occur. In fact, every member of the party takes pride in keeping herself free from accident; it is so like a tenderfoot to get hurt. However, it is well to be prepared in case accidents do occur, and this chapter is intended to forearm you that you may not stand helplessly by when your aid is needed.

Sprains and Bruises
The best immediate treatment for ordinary sprains and bruises is the application of *cloths dipped in very hot water*. This takes out the soreness and prevents inflammation. As soon as one application cools a little, a hot one should take its place, as hot as can be borne without scalding the flesh. Very cold water can be used when hot is not obtainable. For a sprained ankle or wrist continue this treatment for a while and then bind smoothly and firmly with a clean cotton bandage. Keep as quiet as possible with a sprained ankle, and if the accident occurs when on a walk the fireman's lift may be used for carrying the injured person to camp.

The fireman's lift.

Fireman's Lift
To be able to use the fireman's lift may be to save a life, as it can be employed when there is but one person to do the carrying. With practise any girl of ordinary strength can lift and carry another of her own size or even larger. In order to make the lift easy, instruct the patient to relax all her muscles and become perfectly limp; then turn her on her face, stand over her body with one foot at each side, face toward the patient's head. Lean forward and place your hands under her arms, then gently raise her to her knees, next slide your hands quickly down around her body at the low waist-line, lifting her at the same time to her feet. Immediately grasp her right wrist with your left hand, and pass your head under her right arm and your right arm under one or both of her knees, shifting the patient's hips well on your shoulders, rise to a standing position and carry patient away.

Cuts
The accidents that most frequently happen are simple cuts and bruises.
For a slight cut wash the wound in lukewarm water to remove all dirt or foreign matter, then press the lips or sides together and hold them in place with strips of court-plaster or

surgeon's adhesive plaster. Do not cover the entire wound with the plaster, but put strips across at right angles with the cut, leaving a space between every two strips and using only enough plaster to keep the cut closed. Cover the hurt part with a bandage to protect it from further injury.

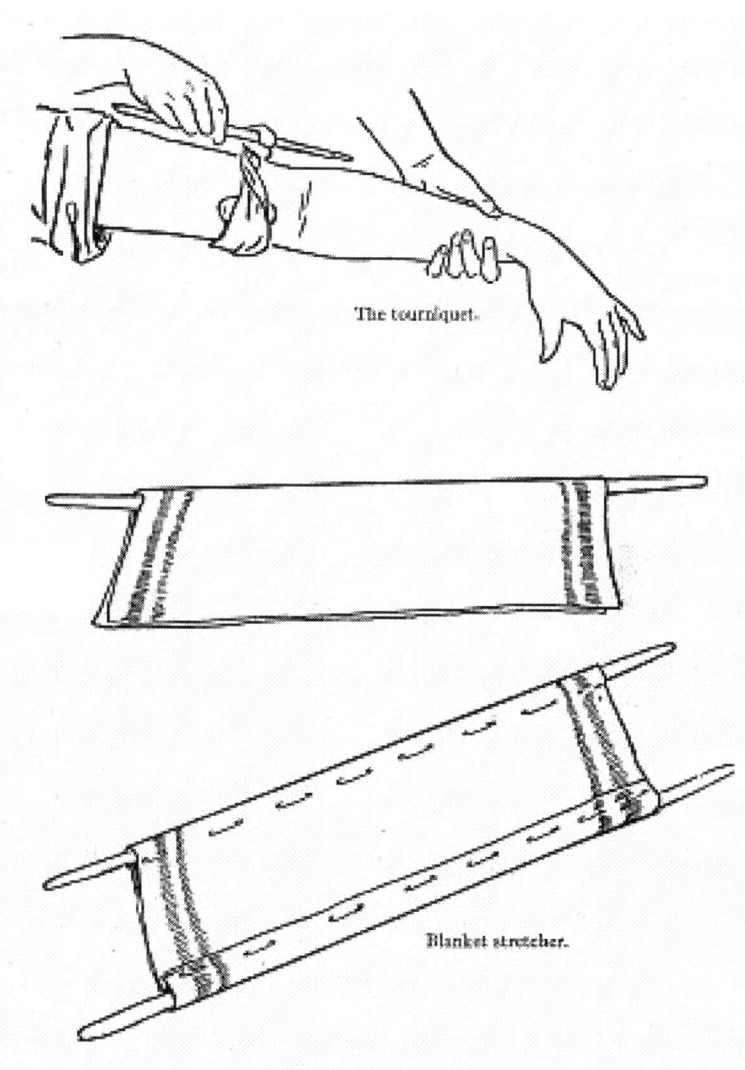

The tourniquet.

Blanket stretcher.

Aids in "first aid."

When an Artery is Cut

When an artery is cut the wound is more serious and the bleeding must be stopped *immediately*. When the blood comes from an artery it is bright red in color and flows copiously in spurts or jets. The blood in the arteries is flowing away from the heart, therefore you must stop it between the cut and the heart.

It is the arteries in the arms and legs that are most likely to be injured. In the arm the large artery runs down the inner side of the upper arm. In the leg the artery runs down the inner side of the upper leg.

The Tourniquet
To stop the bleeding press the artery *above* the wound firmly with your fingers while some one prepares a tourniquet. Use a handkerchief, a necktie, or anything of the kind for a tourniquet; tie it loosely around the limb and in the bandage place a smooth stone (or something that will take its place), adjusting it just above your fingers on the artery. Then slip a strong, slender stick about ten inches long under the bandage at the outer side of the arm or leg and turn the stick around like the hand of a clock, until the stone presses the artery just as your fingers did. Tie the stick above and below the bandage to keep it from untwisting.

Do not forget that the tourniquet is cutting off circulation, and for this to continue very long is dangerous. It is not safe to keep it on more than one hour without loosening. If the hand or foot grows cold and numb before that time loosen the tourniquet and rub briskly to restore circulation. Should the wound begin to bleed again when the tourniquet is loosened, be ready to tighten at once.

In case of an accident of this kind summon a physician, if one can be reached quickly. If not, take the patient to the nearest doctor, for the artery must be tied as soon as possible and only a physician or skilful trained nurse can do that part of the work.

Emergency Stretchers
Loss of blood is too weakening to permit of the patient walking, and the exertion may start the wound bleeding again, so a stretcher of some kind must be contrived in which she may be carried. You can make a good emergency stretcher of two strong poles of *green* wood, one large blanket, and the ever-useful horse-blanket safety-pins. The poles should be about six feet long, of a size to clasp easily in your hand, and as smooth as they can be made with hurried work. They should, at least, be free from jagged stumps or branches and twigs.

Begin by folding the blanket through the middle *over* one of the poles, then pin the blanket together with the large safety-pins, with the pins about six inches apart, to hold the pole in place. That finishes one side; for the other, lap the two edges of the blanket over the second pole and pin them down like a hem. The stretcher will be of double thickness and will hold the injured person comfortably.

If a serious accident should occur some distance from camp and there are no blankets to use, do not hesitate to appropriate for a stretcher whatever you have with you. When there is nothing else cut your khaki skirt into strips about twelve inches wide and tie the ends to two poles (the poles need not be smooth except at the ends), leaving spaces between.

Burns and Scalds
Personally I have repudiated the old method of treating simple burns and scalds and, instead of applying oil or flour, have discovered for myself that simply holding a slightly burned finger or hand in a running stream of cold water not only gives instant relief but prevents the pain from returning in any severity. Care of the injured part to prevent the skin from breaking and causing a sore is the only thing left to be done. However, here are the ordinary remedies for burns. Any of the following things spread over a piece of linen or soft cotton cloth are said to be good: olive-oil, carbolized vaseline, fresh lard, cream, flour, and baking-soda. For serious burns a physician should be called.

Heat Prostration and Sunstroke
This will seldom occur in a camp of healthy girls whose stomachs and blood are in good order, but it is best not to expose oneself to the fierce rays of the sun during a period of intense heat, or directly after eating. In case any one is overcome and complains of feeling faint, and of dizziness and throbbing head, take her where it is cool, in the shade if possible, lay her down, loosen her clothing, and apply cold water to her face and head. She will

probably be able to walk when she revives, but if not, carry her home or into camp. *Do not give whiskey, brandy, or any stimulants.*

Cinder or Foreign Substance in the Eye
As a rule all that is necessary to remove "something" in your eye is to take the eyelashes of the upper lid between your thumb and forefinger and pull the lid down over the lower one. The lower lashes thus shut in, combined with the tears that flood the eye, will clean the eye in most cases.

If the cinder or other substance is embedded in the upper lid, roll back the lid over a match (the sulphur end taken off), then moisten a corner of a handkerchief and with it remove the cinder. If this treatment does not avail and the substance cannot be removed, put a drop of olive-oil in the eye, close it and cover with a soft bandage, then go to a physician. *Do not put anything stiff or hard into the eye.*

Fainting
Fainting occurs most often in overheated and over-crowded places where the air is impure. The proper treatment is to lay the patient flat on her back with the head lower than the rest of the body and feet raised; then loosen the clothes at waist and neck, sprinkle the face and neck with cold water, and hold smelling salts or ammonia to the nostrils. Insist upon giving her all the fresh air possible. It is good also to rub the limbs with the motion upward toward the body.

Drowning—Shafer Method

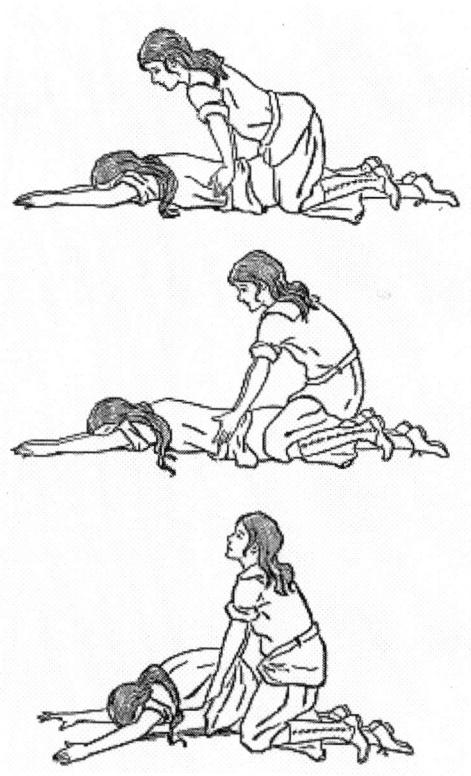

Restoring respiration.

Secure a doctor if possible, but do not wait for him. Do not *wait* for anything; what you do, do *instantly*.

As soon as the rescued person is out of the water begin treatment to restore respiration, that is, to make her *breathe*. If you can do this her life will probably be saved. Not until the patient breathes naturally must you work to bring warmth and circulation to the body. To promote circulation *before* the patient *breathes naturally* may endanger her life.

First quickly loosen the clothes at waist and neck; then turn the patient face downward on the ground with face either downward or turned to one side, arms extended above the head, and with chest raised slightly from the ground and resting upon your folded skirt. Also place something beneath her forehead to raise her nose and mouth from the ground. This will allow the tongue to fall forward. If it does not, grasp it with handkerchief and pull forward; this will permit the water to run out and will provide room for breathing.

As in cases of fainting, so with drowning patient, she must have all the air possible, for she is being suffocated with water, so do not allow a crowd to form around her. Keep every one back except those assisting in the actual work of restoration.

With the patient in the position described, kneel by her side or, better still, astride of her, and let your hands fall into the spaces between the short ribs. With your fingers turned outward and your weight falling upon the palms of your hands, press steadily downward and forward to expel the air from the lungs. Hold this position a fraction of a second, count four, then gradually release the pressure to allow the air to enter again through the throat. Count four, and again press down. Continue this treatment for a while, then, using another method, slip your hands under the patient at the waist-line and lift her up sufficiently to allow her head to hang down as in illustration.

Lower her gently and lift again. Do this several times. You will find that the movement will force the water from the lungs out of the mouth and help to produce artificial respiration.

Return to the first method and continue the treatment until the breath comes naturally. It may be an hour or two before there are any signs of life such as a gasp or slight movement, then the breath must be carefully aided by more gentle pressure until it comes easily without help.

Do not give up hope, and *do not stop working*. The work may be continued many hours if done in relays, that is, several girls taking part, each one in her turn. Remember, however, the treatment must be continuous and no time be allowed to elapse when the change is being made.

After Respiration Begins

With returning breath the first corner in recovery has been turned, but the after treatment is very important. To restore circulation, begin by rubbing the limbs *upward* with a firm pressure. This sends the blood to the heart. Warmth must now be supplied by blankets heated before a fire, and hot stones or bricks may be placed at the thighs and at the soles of the feet. Or the patient should be wrapped in a warm blanket, placed on a stretcher, carried to camp, or to a house, and put to bed. Here hot-water bottles may be used, and as soon as it is possible for her to swallow, if nothing else can be obtained, give a little strong, hot coffee, unsweetened and without milk. Lastly, keep the patient quiet and let her sleep.

Nosebleed

The simplest method of stopping the nosebleed is to hold something *cold* on the back of the neck (a large key will do) and pinch the nostrils together; also cool the forehead with water and hold the arms above the head. This is usually effective.

CHAPTER XIII
CAMP FUN AND FROLICS
Active Sports and Games. Evenings in Camp. Around the Camp-Fire. Quiet Games, Songs, and Stories. Lighting Fires Without a Match

Camp fun should have a place, and an important one, in your plans for the trail. For the time being the camp is your home and it should never be allowed to become dull for want of a little gayety and wholesome amusement. In a permanent camp there will be days when the entire party will be loafing and then is the time to start a frolic of some kind.

Obstacle Races
Competitive sports are always entertaining, and races, of one kind or another, are the most exciting. The Boy Scouts have a race in which the competitors drop first their staffs, then their hats, their neckties, leggins, and, finally struggling out of the blouse of their uniform, they drop that also. All this must be done while on the way and before they cross a given line. At the line they turn to go back over the course and, while running, take up their various belongings and put them on before they reach the home goal.

A race planned on these lines will be most amusing. A smooth course is not necessary, you probably won't have it at camp, and to get over the uneven ground, with the detentions of first dropping, then picking up the articles dropped, will add to the excitement of the sport. An entertaining variation of this will be to have those taking part in the race appear in impromptu costumes (worn over the ordinary dress) which they must remove piece by piece as they run and put the things all on again while returning over the course. Such hastily adjusted costumes cannot help but be funny.

Medals
The winner of the race should be given a medal as a prize. The medal can be made of any handy material. A tin circular disk cut from the top of a tin can will do. Drive a nail through this tin medal near the edge and pass a string through the hole so that it may be hung around the neck of the winner. Or instead of giving a medal, the victor may be crowned, like the ancient Greeks, with a wreath of leaves.

Blindfold Obstacle Walk
Another amusing camp sport is the blindfold obstacle walk. Place six or eight good-sized stones on the ground in a row, about two feet apart. The stones should be flat on top so that you can stand a tin cup filled with water on each stone. Let one member of the party make a trial trip over the cups, stepping between them as she passes down the row; then blindfold her, place two people as a guard, one on each side of her, to hold her hands and prevent a fall, and let them lead her to the end of the line of cups and tell her to go over it again.

The guard will steady her in case she stumbles but must in no way guide her course aright. The stepper will step high and be absurdly careful not to kick over one of the cups, for wet feet would probably be the result. Sometimes the stepper will leave the line of her own accord; sometimes her guard will purposely, and without her knowing it, lead her off the course and then her careful, high steps over nothing add to the fun of the onlookers.

Any number may take part in the sport, and in turn act as stepper. At the end a prize should be given by vote to the one who afforded the greatest amusement.

Hunting the Quail
This is something like the old game of hide-and-seek, with which all girls are familiar, and it will not be difficult to learn. The players are divided into "hunter" and "quails." The hunter is "It," and any counting-out rhyme will decide who is to take that part. When the hunter,

with closed eyes, has counted her hundred, and the quails have scurried away to their hiding-places behind trees, bushes, or rocks, the hunt begins, and at the same time begins the cry of the quails: "Bob-White! Bob-White! Bob-White!" These calls, coming from every direction, are very bewildering, and the hunter must be alert to detect the direction of one particular sound and quick to see the flight of a quail and catch her before she can reach the home goal and find shelter there. The first quail caught becomes hunter in her turn, and the noisy, rollicking game continues as long as the players wish. Another romping game is called

Trotting-Horse

It is warranted to put in circulation even the most sluggish blood and to warm the coldest feet, and it is fine for the almost frosty weather we sometimes have in the mountains.

The players form a circle in marching order; that is, each girl faces the back of another, with a space between every two players. Trotting-horse, the "It" of the game, stands in the centre of the circle. When she gives the signal, the players forming the circle begin to run round and round, keeping the circle intact, while trotting-horse, always trotting, tries to slip between the ranks, which close up to prevent her escape. Trotting-horse must trot, not run. If she runs when making her escape she must go back into the ring and try once more to break away. When she succeeds fairly in getting through the ranks the player in front of whom she slips becomes "It" and takes the place of trotting-horse.

Wood Tennis

Wood tennis is of the woods, woodsy. Green pine-cones take the place of balls; hands, of rackets; and branches, of tennis-net. Lay out a regular tennis-court by scraping the lines in the earth, or outlining the boundaries with sticks or other convenient materials. Build a net of branches by sticking the ends in the ground, and collect a number of smooth, green cones for balls.

Wood tennis must, of necessity, differ somewhat from the regulation game. Since pine-cones will not bounce and there are no rackets for striking them, they must be tossed across the net, caught in the hands, and quickly tossed back. In other respects the rules of the established game may be used entire or simplified if desired.

WHEN DARKNESS CLOSES IN

Around the Camp-Fire
When darkness creeps through the woods, closing in closer and closer; when it blots out, one by one, the familiar landmarks and isolates the little camp in a sea of night, with the mutual wish for nearer companionship, we gather around the camp-fire, the one light in all the great darkness. We are grateful for its warmth, as the evenings are chill, and its cheery blaze and crackle bring a feeling of hominess and comfort welcome to every one. If there are men in the party they light their pipes and then begin the stories of past experiences on the trail, which are of the keenest interest to all campers.

These stories, told while one gazes dreamily into the glowing coals of the fire or looks beyond the light into the mysterious blackness of the forest, have a charm that is wanting under different surroundings. The stories are not confined to the men, for in these days when girls and women are also on the trail, they too can relate things worth the telling.

Songs
Then come the songs. If there is some one in the party who can lead in singing, she can use a familiar air with a rousing chorus as a frame upon which to hang impromptu verses, made up of personalities and local hits. This is always fun and you are surprised how quickly doggerel rhymes suggest themselves when your turn comes to furnish a verse to the song.
The leader begins something like this, using, perhaps, the air and refrain of an old chantey or college song.

Leader
"I spotted a beaver,
But he wasn't very nye."

Chorus
"Don't you rock so hard!"

Second Soloist
"His fur was all ragged
And he had but one eye."

Chorus
"Don't you rock so hard.
Oh! You rock and I rock, and
Don't you rock so hard!
Everybody rocks when I rock, and
Don't you rock so hard."

Third Soloist
"You may laugh at the beaver,
But he's always up to time."

Chorus
"Don't you rock so hard!"

Fourth Soloist
"Oh, do drop the beaver,
And start a new rhyme."

Chorus as before
A song like this may go on indefinitely or until the rhyming powers of the party are exhausted.

Bird-Call Match
In a camp where the members are all familiar with the calls of the various wild birds, a bird-call match makes a charming game when the party is gathered around the camp-fire. The leader begins by whistling or singing the call of a wild bird; if it can be put into words so much the better. For instance, we will take the first few notes of the wood-thrush, which F. Schuyler Mathews has put into notes and words as follows:

Wood-thrush.

Or the yellow-throated vireo, which he gives in this way:

Yellow vireo.

If the leader is correct the next player gives the call of another bird. When a player gives a bird call which is known to be incorrect—that is, absolutely wrong—and some one else can supply the proper rendering, the first player is dropped from the game just as a person is dropped out of a spelling-match when she misspells a word. If there is no one who can give the call correctly, she retains her place. This is excellent training in woodcraft as well as a fascinating game. Your ears will be quickened to hear and to identify the bird calls by playing it; and storing bird notes in your memory for use in the next bird-call match will become a habit.

Vary the Game
You can vary this game by giving the calls of wild animals and the characteristic noises they make when frightened or angry.
Living even for a short time in the wild will develop unsuspected faculties and qualities in your make-up, and to perfect yourself in knowledge of the woods and its inhabitants will seem of the utmost importance. While learning the cries of birds and animals in sport, you will wish to retain them in earnest, and to enter the wilderness equipped with some knowledge of its languages, will open vistas to you that the more ignorant cannot penetrate.

Lighting the Fire Without a Match

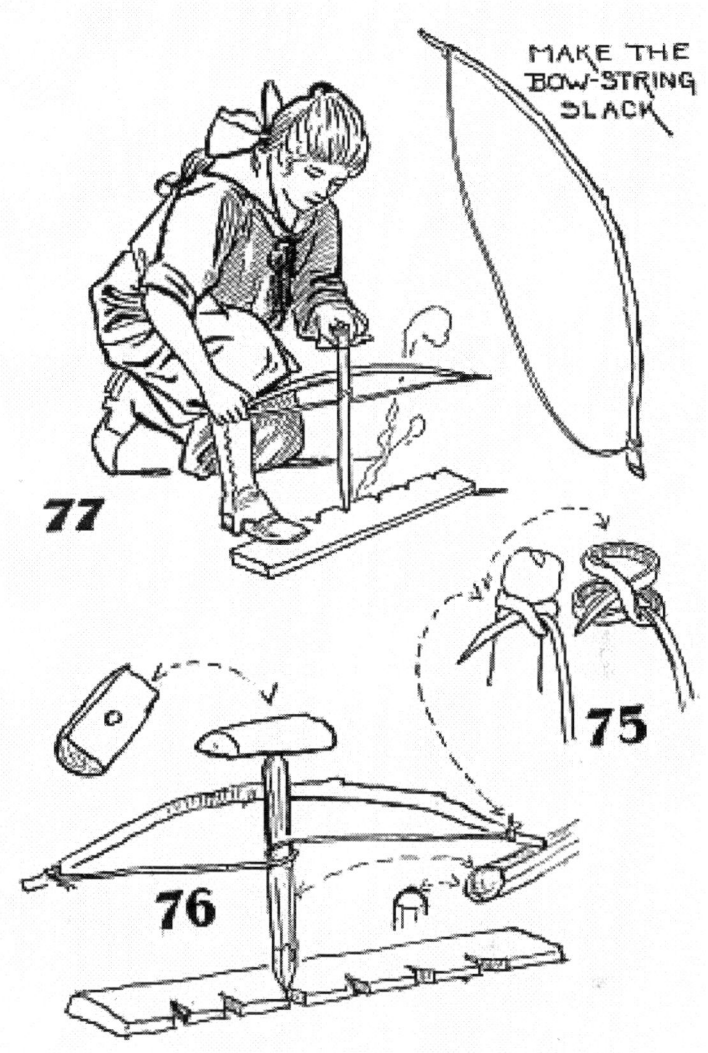

Fire without matches.

A fire-lighting contest is the best of camp sports, for it requires practise and skill, and to excel in it is to acquire distinction among all outdoor people. There are girls in the Girl Pioneers Organization who are as proficient in lighting a fire without matches as any of the Boy Scouts who make much of the feat.

Bow-and-Drill Method
The bow-and-drill method is the most popular among girls and boys alike, and for this, as for all other ways of lighting a fire, you must have the proper appliances and will probably have to make them yourself.
Unlike the bow used for archery, the fire-bow is not to be bent by the bow-string but must have a permanent curve. Choose a piece of sapling about eighteen or twenty inches long which curves evenly; cut a notch around it at each end and at the notched places attach a

137

string of rawhide of the kind used as shoe-strings in hunting-shoes. Tie the bow-string to the bow in the manner shown in Fig. 75, and allow it to hang loosely. It must *not* be taut as for archery.

To the bow must be added the twirling-stick and fireboard (Fig. 76). Make these of spruce. The twirling-stick, spindle, or fire-drill should be a little over half an inch in diameter and sixteen inches long. Its sides may be rounded or bevelled in six or seven flat spaces like a lead-pencil, as shown in Fig. 76. Cut the top end to a blunt point and sharpen the bottom end as you would a lead-pencil, leaving the lead blunt. To hold the spindle you must have something to protect your hand. A piece of soapstone or a piece of very hard wood will answer. This is called the socket-block. In the wood or stone make a hole for a socket that will hold the top end of the spindle (Fig. 76).

The flat piece of spruce for your fireboard should be about two feet long and a little less than one inch thick. Cut a number of triangular notches in one edge of the board as in Fig. 76. Make the outer end of each notch about half an inch wide, and at the inner end make a small, cup-like hole large enough to hold the lower end of the twirling-stick. This is called the fire pit. The reason you are to have so many notches is because when one hole becomes too much enlarged by the drilling of the twirling-stick, or is bored all the way through, it is discarded and there must be others ready and prepared for immediate use.

Tinder

All is now ready for creating a spark, but that spark cannot live alone, it must have something it can ignite before there will be a flame. What is wanted is tinder, and tinder can be made of various materials, all of which must be *absolutely dry*. Here is one receipt for making tinder given by Daniel C. Beard: "The tinder is composed of baked and blackened cotton and linen rags. The best way to prepare these rags is to bake them until they are dry as dust, then place them on the hearth and touch a match to them. As soon as they burst into flame, smother the flame with a folded newspaper, then carefully put your punk (baked and charred rags) into a tin tobacco box or some other receptacle where it will keep dry and be ready for use."

This can be prepared at home. In the woods gather some of the dry inner bark of the cedar, the fine, stringy edges of white or yellow birch, and dry grasses, and dry them thoroughly at the camp-fire.

Mr. Beard also says: "You can prepare tinder from dry, inflammable woods or barks by grinding or pounding them between two flat stones. If you grind up some charcoal (taken from your camp-fire) very fine to mix with it, this will make it all the more inflammable. A good, safe method to get a flame from your fine tinder is to wrap up a small amount of it in the shredded bark of birch or cedar, so that you may hold it in your hand until it ignites from the embers produced by the saw."

With all your material at hand for starting a fire, make one turn around the spindle, with the bow-string, as in Fig. 76. Place the point of the lower end of the spindle in the small hole or "fire pit" at the inside end of a notch in the fireboard, fit the socket-block on the top end of the spindle (Fig. 76), and hold it in place with one hand, as shown in Fig. 77. Grasp one end of the bow with the other hand and saw it back and forth. This will whirl the spindle rapidly and cause the friction which makes the heat that produces the spark. When it begins to smoke, fan it with your hand and light your tinder from the sparks.

Without the Bow

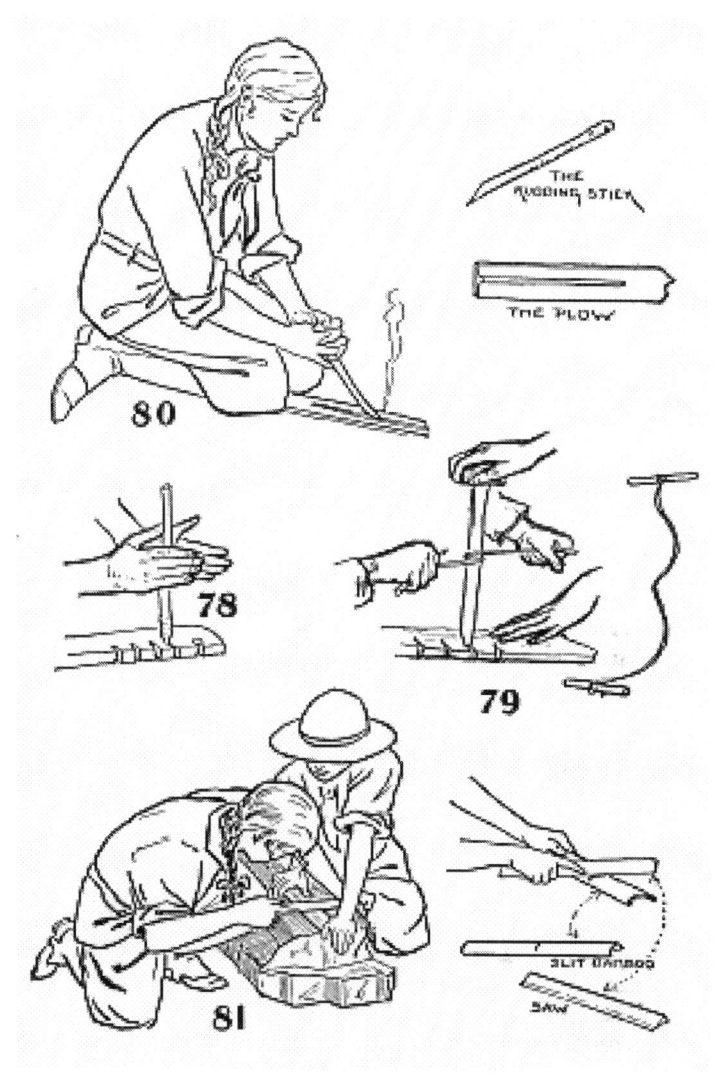

Fire without the bow.

Fig. 78 shows a method which is the same as Fig. 77, the only difference being that the bow is dispensed with, the hands alone being used for twirling the spindle. While simpler, it is very difficult to put sufficient force and speed into the work to produce fire, and it is a very tiresome process. Another way is shown in Fig. 79. It will take two girls to work in this fashion. The spindle is whirled by pulling the leather shoe-string back and forth. One girl holds the spindle and steadies the fireboard while the other does the twirling.

The Plough
It is more difficult to produce fire by the plough method than with the bow, but it can be done. The appliances are simple enough. All you need is a fireboard in which a groove or gutter has been cut, and a rubbing-stick to push up and down the gutter (Fig. 80).

Other woods than spruce are used with success for fire-drills and fireboards, but all must be dry. These are soft maple, cedar, balsam, tamarack, cottonwood root, and *white*, not pitch, pine.

Bamboo Fire-Saw
Part of an old bamboo fishing-rod will supply material for the fire-saw. Cut off a piece of bamboo about fifteen inches long, split it, and sharpen the edge of one piece to a knife-like thinness. Lay the other half down with the curved surface up and cut a slit in it through which the sharp edge of the saw can be passed. One or two girls can work this. When there are two, one girl holds the slit bamboo down firmly, while the other does the sawing (Fig. 81).
Put a little wad of tinder on a dry leaf and arrange it where the powdered sawdust will fall on it. When the powder becomes sufficiently hot there will be sparks and these, falling into the tinder, can be fanned into a flame by waving your hand over it. You will not see the spark but when smoke arises you will know that it is there. Fan gently, else you will blow the fire out, and keep on fanning until your flame is started.

CHAPTER XIV
HAPPY AND SANE SUNDAY IN CAMP
It is a good idea to carefully plan for your Sundays in camp, have every hour mapped out and never allow the time to drag. Make special effort and determine that the day shall be the very happiest day of each week, a day in which every one of the campers will be especially interested and will look forward to with genuine pleasure.
Sit down quietly and think it all out. You will want the day to differ from week-days; you will want it filled with the real life, not half-life, the life only of the physical and mental, but the true, entire life for each camper; you will want to emphasize this higher, inner life, which is the spiritual.
To this end, when you arise in the morning, form the resolution that the day shall be a peaceful, enjoyable one for all the girls. When you take your morning plunge resolve that not only will you be physically clean, but you will also be both mentally and spiritually clean; then all through the day keep in mind that you *can* rule your thoughts and that you *will*, for power to do this will be given to you from the source of all power. Allow not one thought to remain which is not kind, friendly, cheerful, and peaceful. Should other thoughts intrude be firm and severe with them, have no mercy on them, talk to those thoughts as you would to robbers and thieves, tell them to go, *go*, go, BEGONE, that you have nothing in common with them and you *command* them to *go*; then immediately busy yourself with active work, building the fire, cooking, tidying up the camp, etc.
Have your Sunday breakfast especially nice, with a few flowers, vines, leaves, or grasses on the table for a Sunday centrepiece, and keep the conversation on wholesome, happy topics.
After breakfast is over and the camp in order, with all the campers go for a short walk to some attractive spot either by the water or inland, and when the place is reached, having previously selected certain songs containing cheerful, religious elements, ask the entire camp to join in the singing. If one of the girls can sing a solo, let her do so, or it may be that two can sing a duet; then sit quietly while one of the group reads something helpful, interesting, and beautiful, which will be verses from the Bible probably, but may be one of Emerson's essays, or extracts from other thoughtful and helpful writers.
Close the simple exercises with another hymn and return to camp.
In addition to the camp dinner prepare some one dish as a pleasant surprise for the other girls. When dinner is over, the dishes washed, and camp again in order, the girls should have one hour of quiet, to read, write letters, sketch, or lie down and rest. Each camper

should respect the demands of the hour for quiet and rest and *not talk*, but leave her companions to their own thoughts and occupations. If you should see your special friend seated off by herself, do not disturb her during the rest hour; it is each girl's right to remain unmolested at that time.

When the hour is up, the campers can each pack her portion of the evening meal, and in a moment's time be ready to hit the trail, or take the canoe for a paddle to the place previously selected where supper is to be enjoyed, and if the trip be on land, all may play the observation game while on the way.

Observation Game

The leader counts 3 to the credit of the girl who first sees a squirrel, 2 for the girl who sees the second one, and 1 for every succeeding squirrel discovered by any member of the party. A bird counts 6, if identified 12. A wood-mouse counts 4, when identified 8. A deer 20, beaver 12, muskrat 8, chipmunk 10, porcupine 14, eagle 30, mink 16, rabbit 1. The player holding the highest record when reaching the supper grounds is victor. Keep your records tacked up in your shelter to compare with those you will make on the following Sunday.

In this game every time a player stumbles on the trail 5 is taken from her credit; if she falls, she loses 10.

It is a rule of the game that the winner be congratulated by each camper in turn, that she be crowned with a wreath of leaves, grasses, or vines and sit at the head of the table. Keep this game for your Sunday afternoons and play others during the week.

In the evening, as the campers sit quietly around the camp-fire, if the camp director will talk to the girls gently and seriously for a little while on some phase of their real life, the talk will be welcome and appreciated; then just before retiring all should stand while singing the good-night song.

It is hardly possible to present Sunday plans for each variety of camp and campers. The suggestions given are for helping girl campers to look upon Sunday in its true light, and to aid them in working out plans in accordance with the purpose of the day, that they may enjoy happy, sane Sundays in camp.

Note from the Editor

Odin's Library Classics strives to bring you unedited and unabridged works of classical literature. As such, this is the complete and unabridged version of the original English text unless noted. In some instances, obvious typographical errors have been corrected. This is done to preserve the original text as much as possible. The English language has evolved since the writing and some of the words appear in their original form, or at least the most commonly used form at the time. This is done to protect the original intent of the author. If at any time you are unsure of the meaning of a word, please do your research on the etymology of that word. It is important to preserve the history of the English language.

Taylor Anderson

Made in the USA
Columbia, SC
02 June 2025